Brewing Quality Beers: The Home Brewer's Essential Guidebook

(Second Edition)

by
Byron Burch

Joby Books
P.O. Box 512
Fulton, CA 95439

Published by Joby Books, Fulton, California.

Photography by Scott Manchester.
Illustrations by Jeff Reynolds.
Cover photo by Nancy Vineyard.

Printings: 1986, 1987, 1988, 1990, 1991, 1992, 1993

Second Edition Printings: 1993

Manufactured in the United States of America

ISBN 0-9604284-2-9

DEDICATION

To Alicia Laurel, Sierra Joy,
Neva Vineyard and Robyn Sequoia

ACKNOWLEDGMENTS

At the time of the first edition, I said that it was no longer possible to even remember all the people I've traded ideas with over the fifteen years I'd been supplying and teaching brewers. Now that the time has stretched to over twenty years, it is even more true than before.

I must, however, continue to recognize three people from the commercial brewing world who've been especially helpful: Fritz Maytag of Anchor Brewing Co.; Brian Hunt, now of Willett's Brewing Co. in Napa, California; and Gary Bauer, now with Brewer's Research & Development Co.

I also appreciate the various contributions of Jay Reed, who did photography for the first edition; Jay Conner, my business partner from 1978-88; Paddy Giffen and Jeff Anderson, who regularly participate in discussions these days, and who also spent time proofreading the second edition; Scott Manchester who provided additional photography, and Jeff Reynolds, whose line drawings grace this edition as well.

Most of all, credit goes to Nancy Vineyard. Not only did she contribute photographs to the first edition, without her efforts, many of this edition's improvements and expansion would have been impossible. Her first class editorial and layout work are much in evidence throughout the book.

TABLE OF CONTENTS

INTRODUCTION

Welcome to the fascinating world of brewing. It's likely that you already have some appreciation for beer. If not, it's unlikely that you'd be reading this. Probably most of us take for granted the role of brewing (especially home brewing) in human history.

Yet, it's a fact that the oldest known recipe, in the form of a hymn to a Sumerian goddess (and dating back some 5,000 years or so) is a recipe for beer. Indeed, some scholars maintain that the necessity of growing grains for beermaking led directly to the beginning of agriculture, and therefore, was the basis for the rise of civilization itself.

The dominant religions in our part of the world, Christianity and Judaism, first flourished in a wine growing region, and wine furnished some of their most sacred symbolism, but beer was, in many places, revered almost as highly. I've seen at least one devout prayer from the medieval period, in which a nun fervently expresses the pious wish that she could brew an entire lake of beer as a present for God the Father. Such sentiments are seldom heard today, and the language, if nothing else, may be the poorer for it.

Many Americans, in particular, fail to realize that much of the brewing throughout history has been carried out by home brewers. In fact, brewing at home, once widespread, almost became a lost art in the industrialized world, and has really only been rediscovered in the last half of the Twentieth Century.

Many years ago I began *Quality Brewing*, my first book on home brewing, by pointing out that the hobby had gone through many changes since the strange-tasting, bottle-exploding days of prohibition. It was true. Technology and ingredients had made vast improvements and home brewing had moved out of the dark ages. However, those of us brewing back then really thought we'd gone about as far as home brewers would ever go. With a

1

surpassing naivete, we saw ourselves participating in the High Renaissance of home brewing. Little did we know it was only the late Middle Ages that had been reached.

With official legalization in 1979, everything changed. The U.S. Government no longer told commercial brewery people not to share information with home brewers. Suddenly, we found lots of brewers willing to talk brewing. Many suppliers to the brewing industry began to address the home brew market. Soon, the kinds of hops and malt grain varieties available to home brewers was several times what it had been.

In short, though we'd been making very good beers for a number of years, there were now better and more varied ways to do so. With so many possible combinations, the creative challenge was unprecedented, and home brewing emerged as an endlessly fascinating hobby.

After such a spurt of growth, it was apparent *Quality Brewing*, despite it's best seller status, needed to be replaced, and so *Brewing Quality Beers* was born.

The process continues with the second edition.It's now time to incorporate what we have learned over the last 5 or 6 years about new sanitation methods, including the iodophor sanitizers now available. It is certainly time to discuss the advantages of iodophor over either chlorine or sulfite for home brewers. There are, as well, several other important changes to the technology of home brewing that this edition of the book will explore.

For example, my recommended method for handling small amounts of black malt grains has been streamlined, and some of the recipes have been updated to incorporate new hop varieties and malt types. The method for calculating hop bittering units introduced in the first edition has been considerably simplified for beginning brewers, while retaining its essential accuracy.

For brewers preparing to move into all-grain brewing, the advanced brewing sections have been considerably improved and expanded. They now include a number of all-grain recipes for you to try. This edition also takes a good look at using stainless steel "soda kegs" to set up an excellent draft beer system.

In addition, a discussion of water salts will help you to achieve a better match with the world's most common beer styles. Through this kind of disciplined approach to controlling the ingredients in your beer, the advanced brewer will be able to consistently repeat his or her favorite recipes.

As always, my purpose is to assist my fellow brewers (from beginners on up) to make excellent beers. As a beginner, you'll be led through the mixing and boiling of the initial "wort" (your brew before it ferments), and on into the "magical," living, fermentation process which transforms it into finished beer.

If you're a beginner, read through the book up to the section for advanced brewers, and then make up a batch from the selection of ale and stout recipes. After you've made one, read through the book again. Much information will come into focus once you've actually gone through the process and seen how it looks. Although the lager beer recipes are placed at the back of the main text, if you have access to a cool cellar, don't hesitate to brew a pils, even for your first brew. The main difference in brewing techniques, between ales and lagers is the need to keep the temperature cool for lagers, with access to refrigeration a real plus.

Note that a number of unfamiliar terms will be introduced shortly. Don't worry about them. They'll be explained in the text later on. When you've become comfortable with the basic process, make it a point to pick up the book again, and read through the "advanced brewing" section. Some people will want to move on right away, while others will remain comfortable with basic brewing techniques. The hobby cheerfully accommodates both types of brewers.

Note also that this book gives all temperatures in Fahrenheit, with the Celsius reading in parenthesis. If a temperature range is given for fermentation, best results will generally be obtained by striving for the lower end of the range. This shouldn't discourage someone lacking the facilities for temperature control, but be aware that beers can be improved by such control.

Canadian and British readers should also be aware that U.S. measurements are being used. A table of equivalents appears on page 112. Metric equivalents are given in parentheses throughout the text whenever exact measurement is required. There are some exceptions, however, in the advanced section of the book, where including them might have turned the formulae into incomprehensible mazes. Such common measurements as teaspoons, tablespoons, and cups are likely to be part of our households for quite some time, and have been retained.

In the U.S., legalization of home brewing means that (in most states) a single person is allowed to make up to 100 gallons each of beer and wine per year, while the head of a household is allowed 200 gallons of each. Obviously, this formal recognition was very important to the home brew movement, which has grown dramatically in the years since 1978. Most major cities, and a number of smaller ones, now have supply shops for home brewers and winemakers. Check the yellow pages under such headings as "Wine Makers' Equipment and Supplies", "Beer Home Brewing Equipment and Supplies," or "Brewers' Equipment and Supplies." Some firms are equipped to provide mail order service, which will be helpful if you live some distance away.

It's time to get our feet wet and look at the brewing process. We start with the procedure for ales and stouts because these beers are delightful, easy to make, and soon drinkable. We'll look at lagers later on.

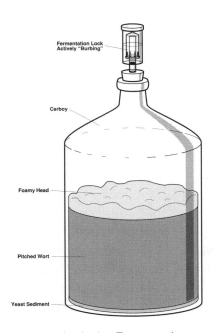

Fermentation Lock
Actively "Burbing"

Carboy

Foamy Head

Pitched Wort

Yeast Sediment

An Active Fermentation.

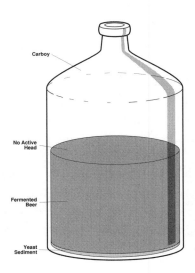

Carboy

No Active
Head

Fermented
Beer

Yeast
Sediment

Ready to rack into bottling tank.

5

PROCEDURES FOR ALES AND STOUTS

COOKING

Start by reading your recipe to see if you will be using any grain malts. If so, start at point "A." If not, skip to point "B."

A. If your recipe calls for one or more grain malts (or other grains), place the cracked or ground grain in a kitchen pan, cover with water, heat to approximately 150° F (66 C.), cover and let stand (either on the stove top or in the oven) for 45 minutes to an hour before you're actually ready to start to work.

Place a colander over your boiling kettle and pour in the grain. Rinse the grain with a tea kettle of hot water, at least 130° F. (54 C.) but not hotter than 170° F. (77 C.), letting the steeping water and rinse water collect in the pot below, until a clear runoff is obtained. Discard the grain. All this liquid collected becomes part of the boil. If unable to fit all the grain into your colander at once, divide it up, and rinse it in stages. Proceed to step B.

B. Thoroughly dissolve any of the following called for in your recipe: Malt Extract, Dry Malt, any Sugar *except* priming sugar, Rice Extract, Dextrin Powder, Gypsum, Salt, Chalk, Epsom Salts, Irish Moss, or Yeast Nutrient, in two or more gallons of water (as much as possible)in your boiling pot. Heat to a rolling boil. Stir in half of the Bittering Hops and boil for 30 minutes, stirring occasionally. Add the rest of the Bittering Hops and boil for 30 more minutes. Finish the boil by adding the Aromatic Hops during the last two minutes.

At the end of the boil, the wort should be cooled as quickly as possible to a temperature between 70 and 80° F. (21-27 C.), so the yeast can be added.

FERMENTATION

Siphon your cooled wort into one or more sanitized plastic or, preferably glass fermentors, leaving most of the sediment behind, filling them no more than two thirds full. Add the Yeast, attach a fermentation lock , and allow fermentation to proceed. In five to seven days at a temperature between 60 and 70°F (16 to 21 C) the yeast will eat the malt and sugar and produce a foamy head on top. When the actively foaming stage of fermentation ceases, the beer begins to clarify and the sample you taste will remind you of dry, flat beer. Now it's time to get ready for bottling.

Glass Fermentor   *Plastic Fermentor*

BOTTLING

Siphon your beer into a sanitized boiling pot (if it's 6 gallons or larger) or plastic bucket, taking care to avoid splashing it. Boil up your Priming Sugar Syrup (See p. 68) and any additional water needed to make the batch up to its 5 gallon volume and stir it in thoroughly. Siphon the primed beer into your bottles and cap them. Check your ales after a week or so. If carbonated, they may be enjoyed immediately, though some will improve with a bit more time in the bottle.

Sit back, then, and enjoy the fruits of your labors. This is what it's all about. The best time to enjoy one of your beers, by the way, is while cooking up a new batch.

Ale and Stout Recipes

LIGHT ALE - 5 U.S. GAL. (19 LITERS)

3 1/2 lbs. (1.6 kilos) Light Malt Extract
2 tsp. Gypsum
1 1/2 lbs. (680 grams) Corn Sugar
1/8 tsp. Salt
1 oz. (28 grams) Bittering Hops (Northern Brewer *or* Perle)
1/4 oz. (7 grams) Aromatic Hops (Willamette, Fuggle
or Cascade)
Water to 5 gallons (19 liters)
3/4 cup Corn Sugar for priming
1 tsp. Yeast Nutrient
1/2 oz. (14 grams) Ale Yeast

> Starting S.G. 1.036 - Final S.G. 1.006-8
> Alcohol by vol. 3 1/2% - Suggested IBU 12-15

PALE ALE - 5 U.S. GAL. (19 LITERS)

5 lbs. (2.3 kilos) Light Dry Malt
or 6 lbs. (2.7 kilos) Light Malt Extract
1 lb. (454 grams) Crystal Malt (Caramel 20)
1 to 2 tsp. Gypsum
1/4 tsp. Salt
1 oz. (28 grams) Bittering Hops (Northern Brewer
or Nugget)
1/2 oz. (14 grams) Aromatic Hops (Fuggle *or* Cascade)
Water to 5 gallons (19 liters)
3/4 cup Corn Sugar for priming
1/2 oz. (14 grams) Ale Yeast

> Starting S.G. 1.044 - Final S.G.1.012
> Alcohol by vol. 4% - Suggested IBU 23-36

BRITISH STYLE BITTER - 5 U.S. GAL. (19 LITERS)

6 1/2 lbs. (3 kilos) Amber Malt Extract
1 lb. (454 grams) Crystal Malt (Caramel 40)
2 oz. (57 grams) 100% Dextrin Powder (optional)
1 or 2 tsp. Gypsum
1/4 tsp. Salt
2 oz. (57 grams) Bittering Hops (Northern Brewer *or* Perle)
or 1 1/2 oz. (43 grams) Bittering Hops (Nugget *or* Eroica)
1/2 oz. (14 grams) Aromatic Hops (Kent Golding)
Water to 5 gallons (19 liters)
3/4 cup Corn Sugar for priming
1/2 oz. (14 grams) Ale Yeast

Starting S.G. 1.050 - Final S.G. 1.012-15
Alcohol by vol. 5% - Suggested IBU 26-30

SCOTTISH STYLE BROWN ALE - 5 U.S. GAL. (19 LITERS)

4 1/2 lbs. (2 kilos) Light Dry Malt
8 oz. (227 grams) Crystal Malt (Caramel 60)
2 oz. (57 grams) Munich Malt (Munich 10)
4 oz. (113 grams) Chocolate Malt
8 oz. (227 grams) Dark Brown Sugar
4 oz. (113 grams) 100% Dextrin Powder
1/2 tsp. Gypsum
1/2 tsp. Salt
1/2 tsp. Powdered Chalk
2 oz. (57 grams) Bittering Hops (Fuggle *or* Willamette)
1 oz. (28 grams) Aromatic Hops (Northern Brewer, dry hopped)
Water to 5 gallons (19 liters)
3/4 cup Corn Sugar for priming
1/2 oz. (14 grams) Ale Yeast

Starting S.G 1.047 - Final S.G. 1.015
Alcohol by vol. 5% - Suggested IBU 23-25

Nut Brown Ale - 5 u.s. gal. (19 liters)

5 lbs. (2.3 kilos) Amber Dry Malt
or 6 lbs. (2.7 kilos) Amber Malt Extract
12 oz. (340 grams) Crystal (Caramel 20)
4 oz. (113 grams) Chocolate Malt
2 oz. (57 grams) 100% Dextrin Powder
1/4 tsp. Salt
1/2 tsp. Powdered Chalk
1/2 oz. (14 grams) Bittering Hops (Nugget *or* Eroica)
1 oz. (28 grams) Aromatic Hops (Willamette *or* Mt. Hood)
Water to 5 gallons (19 liters)
3/4 cup Corn Sugar for priming
1/2 oz. (14 grams) Ale Yeast

Starting S.G. 1.045 - Final S.G. 1.012
Alcohol by vol. 4% - Suggested IBU 22-26

Fruit Ale - 5 u.s. gal. (19 liters)

5 lbs. (2.3 kilos) Weizen (Wheat and Barley) Dry Malt
1/4 tsp. Salt
1/2 tsp. Gypsum
1 oz. (28 grams) Bittering Hops (Northern Brewer)
1/2 oz. (14 grams) Aromatic Hops (Liberty, Cascade
or Hallertauer)
Water to 5 gallons (19 liters)
3/4 cup Corn Sugar for priming
1/2 oz. (14 grams) Ale Yeast
1 to 5 lbs. (1 to 2.3 kg.) Fresh Fruit or Berries. Refer to
pgs xx for instructions for adding the fruit

Starting S.G. 1.045 - Final S.G. 1.008-10
Alcohol by vol. 4% - Suggested IBU 15-18

PORTER - 5 U.S. GAL. (19 LITERS)

5 lbs. (2.3 kilos) Light Dry Malt
or 6 lbs. (2.7 kilos) Light Malt Extract
2 lbs. (907 grams) Crystal Malt (Caramel 40)
1 1/2 lbs. (680 grams) Munich Malt (Munich 10)
4 oz. (113 grams) Chocolate Malt
4 oz. (113 grams) Black Patent Malt
4 to 6 oz. (113 to 170 grams) 100% Dextrin Powder
1/4 tsp. Salt
3/4 tsp. Powdered Chalk
1 3/4 oz. (50 grams) Bittering Hops (Nugget *or* Eroica)
1 oz. (28 grams) Aromatic Hops (Willamette *or* Golding)
Water to 5 gallons (19 liters)
3/4 cup Corn Sugar for priming
1/2 oz. (14 grams) Ale Yeast

Starting S.G. 1.050 - Final S.G. 1.015
Alcohol by vol. 5% - Suggested IBU 45-58

IRISH STYLE STOUT - 5 U.S. GAL. (19 LITERS)

5 lbs. (2.3 kilos) Dark Dry Malt
2 lbs. (907 grams) Amber Malt Extract
1 lb. (454 grams) Roasted Barley
1/4 tsp. Salt
1/2 tsp. Powdered Chalk
1 1/2 oz. (43 grams) Bittering Hops (Northern Brewer)
1/2 oz. (14 grams) Aromatic Hops (Willamette *or* Cascade)
Water to 5 gallons (19 liters)
3/4 cup Corn Sugar for priming
1/2 oz. (14 grams) Ale Yeast

Starting S.G. 1.058 - Final S.G. 1.020
Alcohol by vol. 5% - Suggested IBU 30-35

IMPERIAL STOUT* - 5 U.S. GAL. (19 LITERS)

8 lbs. (3.6 kilos) Dark Dry Malt
1 lb. (454 grams) Crystal Malt (Caramel 90)
8 oz. (227 grams) Black Patent Malt
5 lbs. (2.3 kilos) Rice Extract
1 lb. (454 grams) Corn Sugar
1/4 tsp. Salt
3 oz. (85 grams) Bittering Hops (Northern Brewer *or* Perle)
and 2 oz. (57 grams) Bittering Hops (Nugget *or* Eroica)
2 oz. (57 grams) Aromatic Hops (Cascade)
and 1/4 oz. (7 grams) Aromatic Hops (Saaz, dry hopped)
Water to 5 Gallons (19 liters)
3/4 cup Corn Sugar for priming
1/2 oz. (14 grams) Pasteur Champagne Wine Yeast

> Starting S.G. 1.095 - Final S.G. 1.035
> Alcohol by vol. 7% - Suggested IBU 100-120

*Note that this beer will require several months in the bottle to mature. It will introduce you to a special class of strong beers known as "Barley Wines"

BARLEY WINE - 5 U.S. GAL. (19 LITERS)

8 lbs. (3.6 kilos) Light Dry Malt
3 lbs. (1.4 kilos) Crystal Malt (Caramel 20)
1 1/2 lbs. (681 grams) Munich Malt (Munich 10)
1 1/2 oz. (43 grams) Chocolate Malt
8 oz. (227 grams) 100% Dextrin Powder
2 oz. (57 grams) Bittering Hops (Eroica *or* Nugget)
3 oz. (85 grams) Aromatic Hops (Cascade, dry hopped)
Water to 5 gallons (19 liters)
3/4 cup Corn Sugar for priming
1/2 oz. (14 grams)Pasteur Champagne Wine Yeast

> Starting S.G. 1.105 - Final S.G. 1.030
> Alcohol by vol. 8% - Suggested IBU 70-100

Whole Hops and Pelletized Hops

INGREDIENTS

If you're a beginner reading this for the first time, you're probably bewildered by now by the mass of unfamiliar terms swarming about your head. Don't panic, though, because explanations are coming up starting here. It should also be said, for the sake of reassurance, that once you have brewed one or two batches, the basic process will be rather routine. Thus encouraged, hopefully you're ready for some detailed discussion and advice concerning equipment, ingredients, and those procedures which aren't self-explanatory. We start with the ingredients.

There have been a large number of changes to the quality and variety of ingredients used in brewing in the last several years. This creates a particular need to discuss what they do and why. For convenience, we can group them into seven categories: *malts, sugars, other adjuncts, hops, yeasts, water and water treatment, and optional refinements.*

1.   Malts.   We could lump malts and sugars together as "fermentables." Both provide sugars for the yeast to convert. Malt, however, is a far more complex subject than are the other sugars, and there is a considerable difference in the way it is treated. Barley malt exists at the very heart of brewing. Malt contributes a balancing sweetness and a dry grain flavor when combined with the bitter qualities of hops. Each style of beer that you brew is unique in its composition of malts. Also, body, or more correctly, "full mouth feel", stems, at least partially, from the way the malt is handled.

Most sugars, on the other hand, serve primarily to raise the alcohol level in a given brew while doing relatively little for the body and flavor. Thus, if you prefer full-bodied, richly flavored, beers, you will doubtless want to try brews with a relatively high malt content, severely limiting or eliminating the use of other sugars, except at bottling time.

Though other grains can be malted, most home brewers use the term "malt" primarily in reference to malted barley. In the malting process the grain is allowed to partially sprout. Then it is kiln-dried at lower or higher temperatures, depending on whether a light or dark colored malt is desired. Malting begins the process by which the starches in the grain are converted into fermentable sugars. The "mashing" procedure, in which the grain is crushed, water is added, and the mixture is steeped at particular temperatures for specified periods of time, completes the process.

Fortunately, home brewers don't need to go through all that to brew excellent beers. Reasonably priced, high quality, concentrated extracts of barley malt are on the market in either syrup or powdered form. These are concentrated from malt after it has been mashed, so beginning home brewers are able to brew a bit more simply than would otherwise be the case. For ease in differentiation, I call the concentrated syrups, "malt extracts" and the powdered extracts, "dry malts".

In recent years, most quality malt extracts and dry malts have been those from Britain, with good ones also coming from Germany, Canada, Australia, and the U.S. The list, of course, may change, and when new extracts surface, submit them to exhaustive research.

In any case, light, amber, and dark malt extracts of good quality may now be obtained, and some of the better known brand names have become household words among the American home brewing fraternity. In addition, there are some very good wheat malt extracts on the market, and an excellent dry malt which is a blend of wheat and barley.

Adding modest amounts of grain malts and/or other grains helps to provide additional color or complexity of flavors. To do this, follow the "Simple Infusion Mashing" procedure on pages 62-64. Quite a number of malt grains are now available to home brewers. Here's a discussion of some of the more common ones.

Note that in the U.S., grain malts are classified according to either the "Lovibond" or "SRM" scales. These scales (SRM is the modern version) are essentially equivilent, and refer to the amount of color a given malt is capable of contributing to your beer. For more information about this, see pp. 100-103. Don't worry too much about it, however, until you are ready to move on to advanced brewing. In the following paragraphs, you only need to observe that SRM estimates are given in parentheses. You are likely to find a range of colors available for some types of malts (such as Munich and Crystal). In these cases, my suggestions are indicated whenever these malts appear in recipes.

Pale Malted Barley (3) will be referred to in just about any home brewing text you happen to be reading. A distinction should be drawn, however, between British and American pale malts. British (and Australian) pale malt will be a bit darker, tending to give your beer a gold color. It also has a somewhat different flavor than the American. Domestic pale malt should properly be called Lager Malt.

Lager Malt (1.5-1.8) is extremely light in color, crisp and dry in flavor. If you advance to grain brewing, you will find yourself using it, logically enough, as the base malt for making your very light, delicately flavored lagers, and perhaps in other beers as well.

Either Pale or Lager Malt can be used in small amounts to add body and flavor to any type of beer, or to raise slightly the Specific Gravity of a wort. They are also the primary malts used in most beers made "from scratch" by advanced brewers.

Domestic lager malt can be made from "two row" or "six row" strains of barley. Two row malt commands a slightly higher price commercially because it gives a slightly higher yield. It is usually considered the malt of choice for most purposes. Six row malt, on the other hand, has a higher percentage of husk, which makes it easier for advanced brewers to brew beers that employ grains such as wheat, which have no husk of their own. British or European malts will normally be made from two row barley.

Pilsener Malt (2) is a Lager Malt. Accompanied by certain yeast strains, it tends to contribute a slightly sulfury overtone characteristic of many continental beers.

Mild Ale Malt (4-5) has more color than pale malt, and may be substituted for it when making brown ales.

Munich Malts (5-20) are pleasant, aromatic malts, giving beer a gold to amber cast, depending on the amounts used and their color rating. In many recipes you may substitute some Munich Malt for Pale, Lager, or Crystal Malt for a somewhat different effect.

"Home Toasted Malt" can be made, by the way, by taking some uncrushed Lager Malt, spreading it out on the bottom of a cookie sheet or cake pan to a depth of one inch or less, and toasting it in a pre-heated oven. The effect is somewhat similar to very fresh Munich Malt. I've had good success toasting malt at 350° F. (177 C.) for either 10 or 20 minutes, and also for 20 minutes at 300° F. (149 C.). You may wish to experiment with a variety of toasting programs. (See also pp. 103-104.)

Vienna Malt (4-6) has about the same color range as the lighter Munich Malts. Use it in small amounts as a specialty malt or as the base malt for amber to dark all-grain lagers.

Wheat Malt (2-3) added in small amounts will give your beer a light, clean taste. It is also good for head retention.

Crystal (caramel) Malts are usually kiln-dried at higher temperatures than are the above malts, and this gives them darker colors *(20, 40, 60, 90, 120)* and caramelized flavor. They are used in relatively small amounts for adding color and flavor to amber, brown, and dark beers. Crystal Malts can range from light in color to relatively dark.

It should be noted that the term, "crystal malt," could cause confusion if you're reading American commercial literature. When professional brewers in this country use the term, they're speaking of a somewhat different malt. What we call "Crystal Malt" they call "Caramel Malt". This is because American home brewing has its roots in England, where the term, "Crystal Malt" is used, so this designation has become universal among home brewers, with most suppliers using it in their packaging as well. For this reason I'll stick with it (with reservations).

Black grains are very dark *(400-550)* and strong flavored. They are used in dark beers and stouts, strictly for color and flavor. Unlike the lighter grain malts, black grains do not absolutely have to be mashed, as all the starch has been effectively burned out during the kilning, and they consequently have little effect on the amount of fermentables in your wort.

There are a couple of options as to how to treat black grains. Unless you have a recipe indicating otherwise, you may add black patent malt (and the other black grains) to the boil uncrushed 10 to 30 minutes before the end of the boil. If you do that, tying them up in cheesecloth makes them easier to remove at the end. You may also crush and steep them, either by themselves or separately, according to the "Simple Infusion Mash" procedures on pp.62-64. That will extract the "goodies" you want, even though you're only looking for color and flavor, and not fermentable sugars.

Black Patent Malt (500) gives a straightforward "roasty" flavor, and loads of color for black brews. Black Patent has been available to American homebrewers much longer than any other of the black grains, and for many years, was the only option. Should you have access to recipes from the 1970's, you may wish to try substituting other black grains instead.

Roasted Barley (540) is similar to Black Patent, but is roasted without being malted first. As Roasted Barley is used in Guinness Stout, it should be used in your Irish stouts as well. Technically, it is an adjunct, but it's placed here because it's usage is similar to that of Black Patent and Chocolate malts.

Chocolate Malt (400) is given a slightly lighter roast than either Black Patent or Roasted Barley, and consequently has less color, and a maltier and smoother flavor that is more suitable for porters. Do, of course, experiment with these black grains, blending them in various proportions to suit your own taste.

Several other, less common, malts are available to home brewers these days, and still more will be in the future, but at this point only one more needs particular mention.

Dextrine Malt (1.8), also known as cara-pils or cara-crystal, when added late to a mash, contributes primarily unfermentable dextrins, increasing the full mouth feel of the beer, giving it additional smoothness and sometimes a sense of sweetness as well. Dextrins are perhaps best understood by thinking of them as neither a sugar or a starch, but existing somewhere in between the two groups. They are not considered directly fermentable, though some yeasts may convert them to a fermentable form over an extended period of time. Dextrins are also formed in an ordinary mash, but the addition of up to a pound of dextrine malt to the mash for a five gallon batch of beer, allows you to increase the amount. Extract brewers can get a similar effect by adding dextrin in powder form. *Dextrin powder* is relatively new to home brewers, though dextrins have always played a part in brewing.

When grain malt is mashed, there are two kinds of enzymes at work. One kind converts grain starch into maltose, a fermentable sugar, while the other major enzyme creates dextrins, not directly fermentable, but giving the brew a kind of fullness and a sweet overtone. The first group of enzymes works most effectively at temperatures of 140-149° F. (60-65 C.) The second operates best at 150-158° F. (66-70 C.). If you were brewing from grain, you would vary your mash temperature to create the desired effect. Until a few years back, though, extract brewers had their hands tied because most malt extracts are designed for a standard ratio of fermentability.

The use of powdered dextrin allows you to vary things by creating a fuller, sweeter brew, just as using corn sugar or rice extract allows you to move toward the lighter, drier, American style. If you wish to experiment with dextrin powder, use no more than one or two ounces per five gallons with lighter, more delicate beers, ranging up to eight ounces in heavy, dark beers.

Dextrin powder is added during the boiling of the wort. Note that some "malto-dextrin" products contain only 30% dextrin, and 70% fermentable sugar. If not using 100% dextrin, adjust the amount accordingly.

2. Sugars. Simply expressed, the fermentation process is yeast cells acting on sugars present in the wort, dividing them into roughly equal parts of alcohol and carbon dioxide. Thus the amount of sugars present determines the final alcohol content. In brews where only malt is used, all the alcohol is derived from malt sugar (maltose). In others, when a lighter bodied, less malty beer is desired, or to accomplish particular effects, other sugars may be used to supplement the malt. These other sugars, as well as the grains and other things they are derived from, are known collectively as "adjuncts". Normally, at least 70% of the sugars in your wort will be derived from malt, and no more than 30% from adjuncts, though there are exceptions.

Corn Sugar (Dextrose) is the adjunct sugar most extensively used in home brewing. It is readily fermentable and carries less potential for off-flavors than cane sugar does. The more sugar you substitute for malt in your beer, the lighter in color and taste the beer will be. If you wish to do a relatively light bodied, American style beer, you may use as much as 30% sugar. Note that either corn or cane sugar in large amounts may give your beer a "cidery" taste. If you find this disagreeable, stick to beers with a high malt content, using little sugar, or substitute rice extract for any dry sugar called for in your recipe.

Cane Sugar (Sucrose) will produce a slightly higher gravity, and consequently more alcohol, than corn sugar, but it has a hotter taste when fermented, making it less useful in brewing, particularly as far as the more delicately flavored beers are concerned.

Golden Syrup is a richly flavored, almost "honey-like" syrup made from Cane. It may be used in amounts ranging from two ounces to a pound to add interest to ales, porters, and stouts.

Honey may also be used to excellent effect as an alternative to golden syrup in the same types of situations. In this case, the kind of honey used will have an effect on the character of the beer, with the lightest honeys tending to be the most delicate. Note that more than one pound of honey per five gallons can cause a fermentation to slow down. The addition of an all purpose yeast nutrient helps to keep things moving along.

Milk Sugar (Lactose) is non-fermentable, and can therefore be used to sweeten certain stouts. Lactose does this well, but it has a distinct flavor that doesn't go well with lighter beers. To add smoothness or a hint of sweetness to those beers, use dextrin powder (See pp. 19-20.) Lactose is best added by cooking up a sugar syrup just as you do with priming sugar, though it will not clarify quite as well.

Brown Sugar (or Molasses) can be used in small amounts for flavoring dark ales, the darker versions taste stronger.

Demerara Sugar is a special, light brown sugar from England. It is called for in some British recipes, and can be used to supplement ordinary brown sugar or molasses in many situations.

Treacle is a heavy, black molasses from England. Use in small amounts for complexity in black beers.

3. Other Adjuncts. *Rice Extract* is one of the more interesting adjuncts to come along recently. Some major American breweries use rice as an adjunct to lighten their beers. Rice tends to give beer a crisper, drier flavor than corn does, but until recently you could only use it by first boiling the rice, and then mashing it with barley malt (for enzymes). Rice Extract, however, may be added directly to your boiling kettle, just as you would with malt extract. This means you no longer have to be an advanced "all-grain" brewer to incorporate the flavor profile rice can give your beer.

Note that beers made with Rice Extract may take a bit longer to clarify in the bottle than other beers. To use Rice Extract, substitute it for corn sugar on a pound for pound basis. You'll probably want to use corn sugar for priming, though, because its a lot easier to measure exactly.

There are a number of *unmalted grains* you may wish to experiment with. The easiest to work with are usually those in flaked form because the flaking process prepares the starch for conversion to fermentable sugars when exposed to the enzymes present in barley malt. Because they don't furnish the enzymes themselves, adjuncts such as these should always be mashed with an equal or greater amount of lager or pale malt.

Flaked Rice can be used in place of rice syrup, but the products I've seen have been prone to rancidity, so make sure it is fresh. As with rice extract, and with corn sugar, no more than 30% of the fermentable sugar should be derived from this source.

Flaked Oats can be used if you wish to try your hand at oatmeal stout. Most recipes call for a pound in a five gallon batch.

Flaked Wheat helps with head retention, and provides a bit of grainy character. I would limit the addition for head retention purposes to 8 oz. in a five gallon batch.

Flaked Maize (Corn) or Yellow Corn Grits may be used in the same way and in the same amounts as flaked rice. The effect is different in flavor, but common to most American lagers.

Note that a number of potential adjuncts, including some of the ones just mentioned, are commonly available as breakfast cereals. If using these, read the label and be on the lookout for preservatives. You don't want to make things hard for your yeast, do you?

4. Hops. When brewers speak of hops, they refer to the flower cones of the female hop plant (humulus lupulus). It is these which are harvested, dried, and used in beermaking. Hops in this original flower form are usually called "whole hops."

Hops serve as a preservative in beer, and as a flavoring and aromatic agent. It is useful to distinguish between *"bittering"* and *"aromatic"* hops, due to the timing of your addition to the wort, though in practice most hop varities can be used for either effect. You will also see recipes that refer to *"dry hopping."*

Bittering Hops are so designated because during the preparation of the wort they are boiled with the malt for 30-90 minutes, during which time bitter resins are extracted from the hops, giving a pleasingly bitter flavor to the beer. In practice, some of these hops are boiled the full time, and others are added a bit later. In addition to bitter flavors, hops boiled with the malt afford a measure of protection against potential contaminants.

In addition to whole hops, hop extracts in liquid form are frequently available. Used as directed, they may be substituted for all or part of your bittering hops.

A much superior alternative, however, is the use of hop pellets, a relatively recent development with overwhelming commercial acceptance. Pellets, are pulverized in a hammermill from whole hops, and have nothing foreign added or taken away in the processing. They are compressed to save storage space and are every bit as fresh as the whole cones, though they look more like rabbit food.

You use slightly less with pellets than with whole hops. It used to be common to see whole hops in brown bags sold as fresh hops. These poor conditions led me to recommend using 25% more whole hops than pellets to make up for the losses, but we have seen more consistancy in selling hops from refrigerated or frozen storage, and/or oxygen barrier bag packaging. Consequently, whole hops have been staying in better condition, and I now consider an adjustment of 5-10% less for pellets a better estimate. Pellets are easy to use. They are stirred into the boiling wort in the same way as whole hops, and because they are already powdered they disintegrate and the residue settles out during fermentation and storage. Whole hops are often tied into muslin or cheesecloth bags, to allow for extraction at the end of the boil.

The newest form of hops to arrive on the scene are whole hops (Hop Plugs) which have been moderately compressed into a premeasured form with a set weight (frequently a half ounce or ounce). This can be helpful when you want to do quick measurements. The hops in these plugs are not finely ground like pellets are, and you will need to use a straining bag or some similar method for straining them out of your wort.

Aromatic Hops also play an important role in the making of almost any good brew. They are added to the wort at the end of the boiling process so that their varietal charactistics are maintained. This not only helps a lager to smell "lagerlike," but ales will taste snappier and their fresh hop flavors will counter the heavier malt sweetness usually present in the style. Choose your freshest and most aromatic hops for this purpose.

Dry Hopping is a process of adding aromatic hops to the fermentor after the alcohol is formed to extract a very fresh flavor and aroma. Traditional ales are often dry hopped in cask only days prior to the beers coming on line for serving. Hop plugs work particularly well for this application, but you will still need to remove the hops before bottling or kegging. Remember that British beers are pulled gently from the cask and not pushed with 15 psi of CO_2. You may dry hop with pellets in the secondary fermentor, leave them in the fermentor for several days before racking off and bottling.

One of the most important developments in the past dozen years or so, is a major increase in the variety of available hops. A number of top grade varieties, both domestic and European, have become familiar to North American home brewers. As time goes by, the availability of specific types will probably vary, but here are some we've gotten to know.

Northern Brewer is a superb hop with a clean, almost minty flavor. This is a favorite hop for ales, stouts, and steam beers.

Perle is another excellent mid-range bittering hop with a slightly spicy aroma and flavor, used in most lagers.

Cluster is a variety widely grown in the United States. It rates medium high in bitterness and has a characteristic taste which some home brewers don't particularly care for, but it serves acceptably as a bittering hop in blends.

Brewer's Gold and Bullion are full, but rather coarse flavored, hops. They were once common because of relatively high levels of bitterness. However, newer varieties, such as *Nugget, Chinook, Eroica,* and others, have both better flavor characteristics and much higher bitterness levels, and these two older varieties are in the process of being replaced.

Fuggle has a spicy aroma, though it is quite low in bitterness. It's a good aromatic hop for ales and stouts. It appears to be on the way out, however, with Willamette being the replacement.

Willamette is a newer strain of Fuggle grown in Oregon. Characteristics are similar, but it is much easier to grow than the traditional Fuggle. Has a pleasant nose.

Cascade is a somewhat mild variety with a distinctly floral aromatic quality. Used either as a bittering or aromatic hop in many beers, Cascade blends well with Hallertauer, Tettnang and Styrian Golding. Used as a dry hop in American Pale Ales.

Hallertau, relatively low in bitterness, but with a crisp, spicy aroma, is probably my favorite aromatic hop for light lagers.

Mt. Hood and *Liberty* are quite new, Hallertau-like varieties developed in Oregon. These two have the same characteristics that make Hallertau such an outstanding aromatic hop, and serve as an all-around hop for lager beers.

Tettnang is, like Hallertau, a German hop with similar flavor, but less aroma and may be substituted when available.

Styrian Golding is a spicy hop from Yugoslavia that blends beautifully into many lagers.

Spalt is another German lager hop, not excessively bitter, but with a nice roundness of flavor. It blends nicely with any or all of the last four varieties mentioned. Used alone, it has the earthiness present in German varietals, but without the spiceness of the Saaz.

Saaz is an assertive, Czechoslovakian hop considered by many the world's best pilsner hop.

Centennial, (CFJ90), is an excellent high alpha, very bitter hop with similar aroma to Cascade.

It should be mentioned that this is a very partial list covering only some varieties widely available on the North American home brewing scene at the moment. New varieties are constantly being developed with the best of them going into commercial production. The trend is to increasingly bitter (high alpha acid) varieties.

The recipes in this book suggest particular varieties of hops.

The selections reflect both personal taste and current availability. They are in no way intended as definitive statements. Should you have other varieties where you are, try them out. The recipes only offer suggestions to get you started.

With hops and malts particularly, you will no doubt want to start experimenting as soon as you have acquired a measure of experience and a degree of self confidence. The recipes are good ones, but they've never been inscribed on stone tablets and hand carried down from Mt Sinai, at least so far as I know. Remember that one advantage of home brewing is the potential for arriving at your own personal beer, created by you and answerable only to your individual taste.

Recipes, however, will serve as guidelines that will broaden your brewing knowledge of recognized beer styles. In my experience, the home brewers who derive the most enjoyment from the hobby are those who aren't content simply to brew good beer, but who ultimately move on to explore the various beer styles and to work at the discipline of duplicating them.

As far as hops are concerned, remember that more bittering hops will give you more bitterness, while more aromatic hops will increase the fresh hop flavor and aroma, and that some varieties are more bitter (or more flavorful and aromatic) than others.

Having said that, it's time to explain a bit more about why hops are added when they are. When brewers refer to the bittering potential of a given lot of hops, it is customary to speak of the "alpha acid" content, because that is far and away the most important constituent that the boil derives from the hop.

One major advance for home brewers in the last several years is that virtually all suppliers list the alpha acid content of the hops they sell right on the label. Well they should, because that's what allows us to calculate (as accurately as tolerances of our scales allow) the potential bitterness of what we're brewing, and to be completely consistent from batch to batch. To do that, we need a formula to take the alpha acid content of the hop and convert it into bittering units.

Hop Bittering Units

In the first edition of this book, I laid out a method for home brewers to calculate hop bitterness in a way that took boiling time (an absolutely critical factor) into account. To do this, I took the "International Bittering Unit" (IBU) system, with some commercial assumptions about the extraction of hops in the boil, and simplified some of the math, turning it into a reasonably easy three-step process. In the years since its introduction, it has proven invaluable to brewers all over North America.

Looking back after using and teaching the system for some years, I see a few things capable of further improvement. First, to eliminate confusion, I'm adopting the term "IBU" (the designation used by most commercial brewers.) Second, some of the calculations which follow have been simplified still further so new home brewers can begin using bittering units immediately. Third, I'm always looking for new, or more detailed, information to help improve the suggested ranges in the following chart, so there are a few changes, as well as styles not listed last time.

SUGGESTED BITTERING RANGES FOR SOME COMMON BEER STYLES

Beer Style	*IBU*
Classic Pale Ale	20-40
Bitter	20-35
India Pale Ale	40-60
Altbier	24-30
Light Ale	10-15
Cream Ale	10-18
Mild Ale	15-20

Beer Style	IBU
Brown Ale	15-20
Scottish Brown	15-25
Sweet Stout	15-25
Porter	20-60
Dry Stout	30-75
Czech Pilsner	35-43
German Pils	23-35
American Lager	10-15
Dortmund Export	18-20
Munich Helles	18-22
Vienna/Okt.	18-25
Munich Dunkel	14-24
Bock	25-28
Hellesbock	20-30
Doppelbock	17-27
Rauchbier	20-25
Weizen	13-17
Weizenbock	10-20
American Wheat	10-17

Calculating Bittering Units

There are two reasons to work out the IBUs for any recipe you do, and either one is compelling.

First, even as a beginning brewer, you will very likely find at least one recipe you really like. But without knowing the bittering units, you're going to find brewing it a second time rather a hit and miss proposition, even if exactly the same amounts of all ingredients are used, following an identical procedure. However, by using bittering units, you can get unbelievably close the second time, and anytime therafter.

Second, after you get past the first rush of delight that you, as a new home brewer, can make great tasting beer, you may be ready to move on to the next level of the hobby, which I call "brewing to style". That sort of brewing is a much more demanding discipline, and at that point, a list of suggested bittering ranges for common beer styles will come in especially handy. In the beginning, of course, you may well simply pick out a style you think you might like, and just make sure you start out in the proper range. Even if you don't know the styles yet, you can at least turn guesswork into educated guesswork.

Simple IBUs for Beginners
We're going to assume that the beginning brewer has read and is following the basic instructions in the beginning of this book, adding half of the bittering hops to be boiled for 60 minutes, and half for 30 minutes. The aromatic hops were added with two minutes to boil, and the wort was then rapidly cooled, either in the bathtub, or with a chiller.

To help us with our example, let's use the Pale Ale recipe on page 7. It calls for one ounce of Northen Brewer *or* one ounce of Nugget Hop Pellets, added in two stages as bittering hops with a half ounce of Cascade Hop Pellets added for aromatics, just before the end of the boil. My current stock of Northern Brewer Hop pellets has an alpha acid rating of 7.7%. The Nugget pellets have an alpha acid percentage of 12.6%, and the Cascade pellets are rated at 4.2%.

Grab a small calculator or a sharp pencil and let's figure the bittering units required for the Pale Ale style (20-40 IBU). The important lesson to learn from this exercise and the reason we'll be trying it with two different lots of hops, will be to show how much difference in bitterness you will get with different hop varieties, even though they are used in the same way.

Let's run the calculation for the Northern Brewer Hops first.
For the first bittering addition (boil 60 minutes), multiply the

number of ounces times the alpha acid content of the hops.

One half (oz.) times 7.7 (alpha) equals 3.85.

Each hop addition is multiplied by a factor that adjusts the addition to take into account the boiling time. **For a 60 minute boil, the factor is 4.** *Multiply 3.85 times 4.* The first hop addition, then, looks like this: *.5 x 7.7 = 3.85; 3.85 x 4 =* ***15.4.*** If more than one hop variety goes into an addition, the calculation must be repeated for each variety.

For the 30 minute addition, the factor is 1.4. We have another *one half ounce of Northern Brewer with the same alpha rating of 7.7, with only a 30 minute boil, thus we multiply by only 1.4, instead of 4.* The bitterness of the second addition looks like this: *.5 (oz.) x 7.7 (alpha) = 3.85; 3.85 x 1.4 =* ***5.39.***

You can see how important the boiling time is. Using the same amount of hops with the same bitterness rating contributed less than one third as much bitterness with the shorter boil than with the longer boil. **For aromatic hops (boiled less than 15 minutes or dry hopped) the factor you multiply by is halved to .7,** so that a 60 minute boil extracts more than six times the bitterness that would come from an aromatic hop with the same alpha acid content.

In this recipe, however, the amount of hops, and the alpha acid percentage, are both lower when we get to the aromatics, so we have a new calculation. We have *half an ounce of Cascade rated at 4.2%,* so the bitterness added by the aromatic hop addition looks like this: *.5 (oz.) x 4.2 (alpha) = 2.1; 2.1 x .7 =* ***1.47.***

A summary of the IBU calculation for the "Northern Brewer" version of the Pale Ale recipe from page 7.

Let's add up the totals (in bold type) from the various hop additions. In this case, the profile looks like this: **15.4 + 5.39 + 1.47 = 22.26**. If you look back at the chart, you'll see that this bittering unit level just makes it into the Pale Ale category and would be fine for a lightly hopped version of the style.

Now let's run the calculation for the stronger Nugget Hops.
We have one half ounce of Nugget to boil 60 minutes. Multiply *.5 (oz.) x 12.6 (alpha) = 6.3; 6.3 x 4 =* **25.2.** Our second (30 minute) bittering addition is again one half ounce of Nugget. Multiply *.5 (oz.) x 12.6 (alpha) = 6.3; 6.3 x 1.4 =* **8.82.** Finally, the aromatic hop addition would be the same as in the first example, *.5 (oz.) x 4.2 (alpha) = 2.1; 2.1 x .7 =* **1.47.**

A summary of the IBU calculation for the "Nugget" version of the Pale Ale recipe from page 7.
Add the products obtained in our calculations (the bold numbers): **25.2 + 8.82 + 1.47 = 35.49.** In comparison to the "Northern Brewer" version, the "Nugget" version comes out at the high end of bitterness for the Pale Ale style.

You can use this information to calibrate your beers to suit your own preferences. If you prefer hoppy ales, by all means calculate for the strong end of the scale, but in turn, you can produce a delicately hopped beer from your very first attempt.

Special Notes
The factors given in the preceding paragraphs have been specifically worked out for five U.S. gallon batches. If doing other quantities (such as 10 gallons), you need to do one additional step to adjust the IBUs to the batch size you're working with. *For a 10 gallon batch, the correction is easy and obvious. Simply divide the IBU calculation by two and you've got it.* Others may take a little more thought. Divide by the ratio of your batch size to five gallons. Eight gallons, for example, is 1.6 times five gallons, so divide by 1.6. Three gallons is .6 times five gallons, so divide by .6, etc.

Of particular interest to Canadian and British brewers, will be *the correction for six U.S. gallons (Divide by 1.2)* because six

U.S. gallons is the same as five Imperial gallons.

When your brewing has progressed to the point that you're really trying to duplicate past recipes, a major hurdle to overcome is that the alpha acid percentages of hop varieties are quite variable, depending on how the growing season went, where they were grown, etc., so you need to know how many ounces to use when the alpha rating has changed. There is an easy way to do this.

You need to know the ounces of hops, alpha acid percentage, and IBU level of the original recipe. *Simply take the original alpha percentage and divide it by the one for the new hops. Multiply the result by the number of ounces used in the original recipe.* The answer tells you the number of ounces of the new hops you will need to maintain the same bittering unit level as before.

Odd Boiling Times

If you have recipes that call for bittering hop boiling times other than 30 and 60 minutes, and want to really be accurate about what you're doing, you may do so by employing the slightly longer calculation set forth in the last edition.

(A) Multiply the number of ounces of hops by their alpha acid percentage. **(B)** Divide the result by 7.25. **(C)** Multiply the result by one of the following figures, depending on the length of time the hops are boiled. If the hops are boiled 45 minutes to an hour, multiply by 28-30. If the hops are boiled 15-40 minutes, multiply by 8-12. If the hops are boiled less than 15 minutes or are dry hopped, multiply by 5. Add the products of each calculation together to find the total IBU for that recipe.

5. Yeasts These, of course, are the living organisms that makes the whole brewing process work. The yeast you use, therefore, should be selected with some care. The basic rule here is to use only a good quality, active beer yeast.

Baker's yeast should only be used if there is absolutely no

alternative. The fact that many old recipes call for it is inevitable, as it is only recently that beer yeast has become widely available. It is also true that beer yeast and baker's yeast descend from the same ancestral strain, S. Cerevisiae, and that both baker's yeast and ale yeast are still officially designated by this same term, but this is misleading. By means of mutation and selection over millions of yeast generations, the two industries have evolved yeasts vastly different in character.

Beer yeast, for example, can be used in making bread, but it would probably take up to five or six times as long for the bread to raise. By the same token, baker's yeast, used in brewing, tends to ferment at an erratic pace, and often lends a strong, yeasty flavor to the beer. It settles out poorly, and that which does settle is easily disturbed when the beer is poured. Beer yeasts can be purchased inexpensively enough that no one should still be sabotaging their product with an inferior yeast.

One more cautionary note is necessary. Brewer's yeast, as sold in bulk by health food stores, has been deactivated (killed) and will not work. Any fermentation you happen to get will stem from "wild" yeasts of undetermined character.

The topic of yeasts is a rather involved one. For example, I recall reading a few years back that there are 65 recognized sub-strains of lager yeast alone. By now there are possibly more. For our purposes, it will suffice to distinguish between ale yeast and lager yeast. These are commonly referred to as "top fermenting" and "bottom fermenting" respectively, though this distinction is often more traditional than accurate. Few, if any, dried ale yeasts are, in fact, true top fermenting yeasts. Bottom fermenting ale yeasts are often used for making ales commercially as well.

A more meaningful distinction between ale and lager yeasts is that ale yeasts are generally hardier and more vigorous, but lager yeasts are hardier under cold conditions. Thus, ale yeasts should be used if fermenting above 60° F. (16 C.), but lager yeast if fermenting below 55° F. (13 C.). In between, you may use either.

There are, of course, likely to be some differences in the flavors produced by any two yeasts, not only between the strains, but within the classifications as well. This means you'll probably have to do some controlled experiments to see which you like the best. Personally, I like to make 10 gallon batches, split them up, and ferment with two different yeasts. Or you can do essentially the same thing by following the same recipe and procedure with successive batches, varying only the yeast.

It has always seemed to me that lager yeasts settle and stick to the bottom better than ale yeasts, but this may just be because lager beers are usually given more bottle time than ales, giving the "cake" a better chance to form.

One thing that should be stressed is that you should make sure to get what you pay for. "Beer Yeast", especially if packed in Britain, is almost certain to be an ale yeast. To be sure of getting a lager yeast, always look for the specific words, "Lager Yeast", "S. Carlsbergensis," or "S. Uvarum" on the package. Note that fermenting a lager yeast much higher than 55° F. (13 C.) may cause the beer to take on "ale-like" fruity characteristics.

Note also that yeast strains have a "maximum alcohol tolerance", and many will stop working once the alcohol level gets to 8% or 9% by volume. The tolerance level varies, but for beer yeasts it is considerably below the level for wine yeast strains. To be safe, if you have a starting S.G. of 1.070 or above, you may wish to switch to a wine yeast, preferably a hardy strain such as "Pasteur Champagne."

Beer Yeasts in Liquid and Dry Form

The majority of home brewers use dried beer yeasts, and there are some decent ones on the market. These are handy, generally have a good shelf life, and start readily when used at the rate of 1/2 ounce (14 grams) per five gallons of wort. Recently, several commercial quality, laboratory pure, liquid yeast cultures have found their way into home brew supply shops, and while these are relatively expensive, a number of them have proven to be superior to available dried yeast strains, in part because dried yeasts are almost inevitably contaminated with other yeast strains and bacteria in one way or another in the drying process.

Hopefully, the number of pure strains available in liquid form will increase significantly over the next few years, giving us increased flexibility. If using a liquid yeast culture, make doubly sure to aerate the wort by splashing it when putting it into your fermentor. Also, with liquid yeast cultures, you must make a yeast starter in advance.

Yeast Starters

A yeast starter is made up two to three days prior to boiling up your wort. Dissolve about 3 tablespoons of dry malt or malt extract in a pint or so of warm water. Add a pinch of yeast nutrient, heat to boiling, and boil for at least five minutes. When the mixture has cooled to around 80° F. (27 C.), pour it into a small, sanitized jug, filling it no more than two thirds full. A 1.5 liter wine jug or magnum bottle is ideal for yeast starters. If brewing a strong beer (barley wine, imperial stout, etc.), add enough malt and water to bring your yeast starter up to a full quart.

Shake up your liquid yeast culture to pick up the yeast sediment on the bottom, and pour it into the jug. Attach a fermentation lock, and put the starter in a somewhat warm location, ideally between 70 and 80° F. (21-27 C.), and leave it until it starts working actively. If more than four days go by under good conditions with no sign of action, pour off a bit and taste it. If it isn't sweet, it snuck past you while you weren't looking and is done. Should you have a starter ready, but something keeps you from brewing, put the starter in your refrigerator. You may keep it up to four days or so that way.

One recent development is the dual envelope liquid yeast culture. These packages have the yeast in a sealed outside envelope, and a nutrient broth "starter" inside. Striking the package causes the inside envelope to break and the package to swell. Several strains currently packed that way are really outstanding, but they tend to be slow starting unless grown up more than by just swelling the pack. Follow the above instructions after you swell the pack, and give the culture a good 24 hour head start before pitching into 5 gallons.

6. *Water and Water Treatment.* There are many types of water supplies, of course, and these will be variously suitable for brewing. Even an excellent brewing water will be better suited for making one type of beer than another. Generally speaking, brewing water should have a good clean flavor. Avoid water that is high in iron, it can make the flavor of the beer harsh and prevent a head of foam from building. If your supply is strongly flavored, you may decide to use bottled spring water for your brewing, partially or entirely. If you're a beginning brewer, that's probably all you should concern yourself with until you've made a few batches. Then come back to this.

Within a given classification, the lighter the beer, the harder the water; with ales taking harder water than lagers. An exception is Czech-style pilsner, which is made with soft water. Most black beers, including stouts and porters, are best made with water high in "temporary" hardness.

Water, obviously, is about as complex as any subject could be, but to start with, let's concentrate on understanding the three main types: "permanently hard water", water high in "temporary hardness", and "soft water". Another way of saying this is, "water high in sulfates, water high in carbonates, and water low in both." Those of you with a "municipal" water supply have it relatively easy. You can simply call your water company and ask them which you have. Often you can have a somewhat detailed printout sent just for asking. If you rely on a well, as I do, you'll have to figure things out for yourself.

The easiest way to distinguish between hard and soft water is to observe whether or not soapsuds form easily and profusely, a sign of soft water. As far as temporary hardness is concerned, look at your tea kettle. Waters high in carbonates or temporary hardness will precipitate a lot of white "scale" when boiled.

As far as corrections are concerned, hardening soft water is the easiest. Simply adding a bit of Gypsum (calcium sulfate) normally does the trick. Calcium also helps give the yeast an extra boost. In the case of pale ales or British "bitters", you may also wish to add a very small amount of Epsom Salts (magnesium sulfate), no more than a third of a teaspoon for five gallons.

Very hard water is ideal for pale ales or bitters, but if you have that kind of water, you may have a hard time making some other types of beers at their very best. When you want to make pilsners, you may want to use some de-ionized water in the batch. The percentage you prefer may have to be determined by trial and error until you can take a closer look at your water. (See pp. 97-99)

Water with high temporary hardness (carbonates) is not really desirable in most pale beers. Pre-boiling your brewing water, and siphoning it away from the precipitate will remove carbonates. Some temporary hardness is desirable, however, in stouts, porters, Munich style dark beers, bocks, and doppelbocks.

Soft water would be ideal for Czech style pilsners. If you don't have soft water, you can substitute partially with de-ionized water, available at most supermarkets.

Small amounts of table salt may be added to many beers to give them smoothness and fullness, but caution should be exercised not to use excessive amounts.

7. *Optional Refinements.* As you might expect, this is rather a catch-all topic, covering things which don't fit neatly into other categories, but which can be helpful nonetheless.

Yeast Nutrient, Yeast Food, Yeast Energizer, or Brewing Salts can be added during fermentation. As the variety of names suggests, there are quite a few of these preparations available from various suppliers, and the precise formulations are as individual as the names. A teaspoon or so of one of these products, added prior to pitching the yeast, can help speed the onset of fermentation, and also help prevent "stuck fermentations", that can occur when using honey as an adjunct.

Flavorings of various sorts may be added when you are brewing "specialty" or "novelty" beers. These may consist of *fruits, berries, herbs, spices*, etc., in just about any combination. Your personal taste and the breadth of your imagination are the only limiting factors.

In general, *spices* should be added during the last 5-10 minutes of the boil. Fruits and berries may be added at the end of the boil as well, or else tied up in a nylon straining bag and placed in the fermentor. In this latter case, you must ferment in a container with a wide mouth, so you can easily extract the bag when you're ready to remove it.

A number of *natural fruit flavoring extracts* are available, either at home brewing suppliers, or at grocery stores, which you may also find useful in developing your creativity. Some brewers prefer to work this way because flavorings can more easily be handled in a sanitary manner than can fresh fruit.

Pectic Enzyme is added to the wort prior to fermentation when brewing fruit or berry beers. This is a pectin degrading enzyme (antipectin). It is needed because pectin can form colloidal chains that keep fine particles from settling out. The resulting haziness will not only be aesthetically displeasing, but can, in some cases, affect the flavor as well. Add half an ounce of pectic enzyme per five gallons of wort.

Polyclar AT (PVPP) is a proprietary product used to help precipitate unwanted proteins in all-grain beers. Add one gram per gallon to the fermentor just before siphoning in the wort, but at least 15 minutes before adding yeast. If yeast is present, it will cling to the Polyclar, keeping the protein away from it.

Irish Moss, actually a seaweed, is also used to get rid of proteins. It is added to the boiling kettle at the beginning of the boil to help with the "hot break", a coagulation and settling of unwanted protein. You probably won't need to worry about this until you begin using significant amounts of grain. I've seen two forms marketed; flaked, and powdered. Use 1/2 teaspoon of the powdered, or a teaspoon of the flaked variety per five gallons of beer.

Lactic Acid is often used to slightly lower the pH of the "sparge" (rinsing) water when brewing all-grain beers. Two teaspoons of 85% Lactic Acid is generally sufficient for five gallons of water. Stir well.

Ascorbic Acid (Vitamin C) may be added to beer after fermentation as an anti-oxident. Half a teaspoon in five gallons is sufficient. Its purpose is to protect the beer against the air trapped in the bottle or aging tank. This is a particularly good idea if all or some of the beer will remain in storage for some time before being consumed. Note that only pure ascorbic acid should be used. Vitamin C tablets contain only small quantities of the pure stuff, supplemented with a lot of unknown buffers which could leave you with an insoluble, cloudy haze in your beer.

Fining Gelatin and Grape Tannin may be used for a process called "fining", which some writers insist can give your beer more clarity than the unaided settling process can provide. I have traditionally made fining an option since some other authors have made it a requirement. I've never been able to tell much difference in most well made beers.

At the point when you are putting your beer into the settling tank, stir a teaspoonful of unflavored gelatin (75 bloom: grade B) into 10-12 oz. of water (about one large water glass), and let it stand for a half hour. Siphon your beer into an open container. Heat the gelatin and water to 180° F. (83 C.) and stir until the gelatin is dissolved. Stir it directly into the beer, and siphon the beer into a closed container for aging. The gelatin will combine with tannin, provided by the hops, and settle out impurities. Stirring in 1/4 teaspoon of grape tannin before adding the gelatin can be beneficial to the process. The settling process will take approximately one week. Do not repeat.

A Heading Agent may be used to give your brew a longer lasting head when poured than is otherwise possible. A number of such preparations have come into use by commercial breweries, especially since detergents, widely used for cleaning glassware, destroy the head retaining property naturally present in beer. Whichever heading agent your supplier stocks, use as directed.

Isinglass is used frequently in British recipes and is widely available in North America. It is a natural product, the swim bladder of the sturgeon fish. This is dried at harvest and ground to a fine powder. Before you add it to beer, it must be conditioned with an acid, such as Citric or Tartaric, or the winemaking standard Acid Blend. A tablespoon of isinglass powder is soaked in 2 cups of water with 1/2 teaspoon of one of the above acids for 30 minutes. It is next added to the beer during racking from the first container, right at the end of fermentation.

Isinglass will settle protein and yeast to the bottom of the fermentor, which you can than rack away from, four or five days later. Should you use it in conjunction with lagering, you may need to add some fresh, active yeast to the bottling vessel with the priming sugar, as the settlings will have stripped out much of the original yeast.

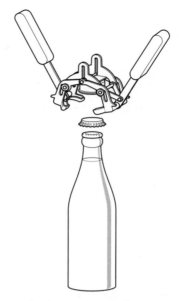

Bottle Capper, Bottle and Cap.

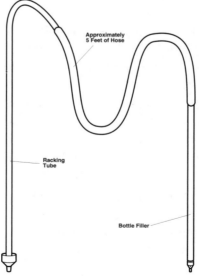

Racking Tube with Bottle Filler.

NECESSARY EQUIPMENT

At least as important as the ingredients you select are the tools that make brewing a pleasure instead of a chore. You should keep two things in mind when choosing equipment.

Good quality tools will save you money in the long run, and though listed as options, the supply list of "optional equipment" that follows this section, includes tools that save you time, adding to your enjoyment of the hobby.

1. A Boiling Kettle. This should be an enamel or stainless steel kettle of at least four gallon capacity. If possible, get one that is at least six to eight gallons so you can boil the entire wort at once. This will help with sanitation, among other things. If not, get two four gallon kettles, and split up the batch.

If that's not possible, you'll have to boil some water with the malt and hops, making up the difference at the end with water that has been boiled previously. The primary disadvantage of this method is that when the wort being boiled is highly concentrated, the amount of "goodies" extracted from the hops is reduced proportionally. In other words, if you only boil half the wort, you should add twice the hops called for to make up the difference. The wort will also darken in color due to the concentration of sugar.

2. Fermenting and Bottling Containers. The most popular and plentiful container for fermentation has to be the old standby, a 6 to 10 gallon plastic food-grade bucket. Thousands upon thousands of them are in use all over North America. They are inexpensive, sound vessels that don't break easily and have a large opening for removing steeping bags of dry hops or fresh fruit. During fermentation, they are covered with a tight fitting lid that allows the gas to escape through an airlock attatched to the lid. The disadvantage of a plastic fermentor has to do with how porous the material is, allowing bacteria to build up on their surfaces in scratches that develop over time. Their large opening also increases the surface area of the beer that is in contact with air, potentially oxidizing the beer below.

The next most popular fermentors are carboys, three, five or seven gallon glass vessels with narrow (1") openings. The advantage of these fermentors is the ease with which the fermentation itself can be observed, and the narrow openings cut down on potential oxidation. Because the surface of the glass is much harder than plastic buckets, it will be easier to clean and sanitize properly. The disadvantage of glass is that it is breakable and care must be exercised when moving them around. The addition of a crate, carboy handle or net increases the safety factor when handling full jugs.

3. A Large Stirring Spoon. Stainless steel is best, but a wooden paddle may be employed up through the boiling of the wort.

4. Fermentation Locks. You will need a fermentation lock for each jug-type fermentor, as well as any bucket fermentor using a tightly fitting lid. They are also called "air locks" or "bubblers", and are available through any winemaking or brewing supplier.

Fill to Line
With Water
(half full)

The inexpensive, plastic, cylindrical type is probably best because it's the easiest to clean. The fermentation lock is partially filled with water so that the bottom of the interior sleeve will remain covered at all times. When you are fermenting in a refrigerator with the cooling element at the top, vodka should be used instead of water so the lock won't freeze.

Fermentation Lock

Wine jugs with standard screw-top threads can be fitted with a screw-top holder for the lock. Other gallon jugs will normally take a drilled #6 rubber stopper. Most glass five gallon "water bottles" will use a #6 1/2 or #7 stopper. Unfortunately, there is variation, even among these common jug types, so if you have a jug at home, measure the diameter of the opening before shopping for a lock and stopper. It may save you a trip to the store.

5. A Siphon Assembly. You will, at some point, need to siphon your brew from one container to another. A five or six foot length of clear, plastic, 3/8" or 5/16" i.d. hose with a stiff, "racking tube" attached to the incoming end and a hose clamp near the other makes an excellent setup. The stiff tube keeps the hose from curling up as it goes to the bottom of the container you're siphoning from. *Note that, from the time fermentation begins, all the way up until your brew is in the bottles, you should avoid mixing any more oxygen into it than necessary.* Therefore, make sure your hose goes all the way to the bottom of the container you're siphoning into so splashing is minimized. This is still true at bottling time, which is one reason you should purchase a bottle filler, a device which will be discussed later.

6. A Saccharometer. This is a hydrometer designed to measure by weight the amount of sugar in a given solution. A small amount of beer or wort is drawn off into a testing jar (graduated cylinder). The saccharometer, an elongated, hollow, glass instrument weighted at the bottom and calibrated along the stem-like upper part, is placed in the liquid, spun around to dislodge air bubbles, and allowed to float freely. When it stabilizes, a reading is taken right at the surface of the liquid, at the bottom of the "meniscus", the slight clinging of the solution to the sides of the saccharometer and test jar.

Since sugar is heavier than water (though alcohol is lighter) a saccharometer, which has a constant weight, will float higher in a sugar solution (such as unfermented wort) than in plain water or an alcohol solution. The more sugar there is, the higher it floats.

The saccharometer's main function in home brewing is to measure the amount of sugars present in the initial wort which allows you to estimate in advance the potential strength of your brew. The inital reading should be recorded and saved.

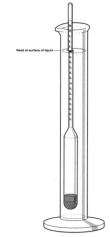

You subtract the final reading, taken at bottling time, from the first reading, to arrive at the amount of sugar that was reduced to alcohol. Next, divide the total by 8 to get an approximate alcohol (by volume) equivalence. In short, a saccharometer allows you to be more exact about what you are doing, and to better understand your hobby.

Saccharometer with Test Jar.

Saccharometers can be calibrated according to the Balling (Brix) scale or the Specific Gravity scale. Though Balling is used in the wine and beer industries, Specific Gravity is a more exact scale and it is used here for that reason. Many saccharometers come calibrated with both, along with a potential alcohol scale. This last can be especially useful in calculating a beer's strength. Just turn to this scale, and subtract the final reading from the first one without having to look up the table of equivalence.

On the Specific Gravity scale 1.000 is the weight of water, with higher numbers indicating additional weight, such as in sugar solutions. Because the range brewers are concerned with primarily involves the two right hand places, you will commonly see it referred to as: S.G. 1.000 = "zero", S.G. 1.035 = "35", S.G. 1.045 = "45", and so on.

If your saccharometer only gives the Balling scale, use the table on page 110 to make the conversion to Specific Gravity.

Note, of course, that if you are taking a reading before all the water has been added to a five gallon batch, you will need to adjust your readings. Thus, a specific gravity of 50 with four gallons of water added would be 40 when the fifth gallon was included. To get the actual reading in this situation, multiply the reading by the number of gallons actually present and divide the result by the total number of gallons it will eventually have. This adjustment is also necessary for final gravities.

Note also that wort used for a test sample should not be returned to the batch, so chances of contamination are minimized.

If you are making your first batch or two of beer from a premeasured kit, you may be able to put off buying a saccharometer temporarily. If doing this, you must rely completely on the absence of visual signs of fermentation (no bubbles rising), and tasting a sample of the beer (it shouldn't be excessively sweet) to tell you when fermentation is done. You should, however, purchase a saccharometer and test jar as soon as possible.

7. A Thermometer.. An immersible, wide-range, dairy type thermometer with a range of roughly 20-200° F. (-7 to 94 C.) is excellent. However, you may wish to invest in a metal probe thermometer (either dial or digital) which will give you a much faster reading.

8. A Siphon Starter. For reasons having to do with sanitation, many brewers are understandably reluctant to suck on the end of their hose to start their siphons. There are a couple of options for those using 5/16" hose, and one for those using 3/8" hose. The first two are very similar in concept, a bulb type baster, mentioned elsewhere as a useful sample taker, can be inserted into the end of the siphon with the bulb wadded up. When it is released, air rushes into the expanding bulb, and starts the siphon flowing. An aspirator, sold in drug stores for cleaning babies' noses, can work also.

Unfortunately, many basters or aspirators I've seen are a bit too small to get the siphon started with 3/8" i.d. hose, but a 60 to 80 cc plastic syringe works nicely. Pull the plunger all the way out, and that will generally suck enough liquid to get things started. Using 5/16" hose makes siphon starting easier.

9. Bottles. Get good, cappable bottles of brown or green glass. Exposing beer to either direct sunlight or flourescent lighting can severely damage it, giving the beer a distinctly skunky smell (Think about the flourescent lights next time you look at the beer display in your local liquor store).

In general, brown bottles afford your beer the best protection, and green less (though more than clear, which gives none at all). The trade-off is that it's easier to see the fill level in green bottles than with brown bottles when you're bottling, so you'll have to make your own decision based on your circumstances. Even if you have flourescent lights in your brewery, if the filled bottles are stored in cardboard cases, green bottles may be used. In any case, get the sturdiest bottles possible that take a crown cap.

Note that you should cover your glass carboys with a cardboard box or blanket if they will be exposed to sunlight or flourescent lights.

Another consideration is the size of the bottles. Large bottles make bottling easier. However, bottle conditioned beers contain sediment, and tipping the bottle back upright will stir up an unnecessary amount of it. Therefore, don't use bottles larger than you intend to pour at one time. If you like large bottles, and can no longer find cappable quart bottles in your area, note that most domestic champagne bottles are designed to take a crown cap, and being roughly 4/5 quart, they are quite useful.

Over the years, I've had a few people tell me that they reseal screw-cap bottles with good success, but many complain that they lose at least some seals.

The clip-top bottle, sealable without a capper, has made a comeback in recent years, and can be used by home brewers, although those with ceramic tops have recently been outlawed in California for reasons having to do with recycling. If you use clip-tops, you will need to replace the rubber gaskets from time to time. Your home brew supplier carries replacements.

10. A Bottle Brush. Helpful in the recycling of old bottles.

11. A Carboy Brush. This is a large brush, long enough to reach the bottom of the jug, and bent near the end so the jug's shoulders can be easily cleaned. You may not need one of these while making your first brew, but you'll probably find it essential in getting ready for your second.

12. A Capper and Caps. Cappers come in a wide variety of styles. Get one that is durable, and that will work on the type of bottles you intend to use. Not all cappers will accept all bottles. If you wish to use champagne bottles but find your capper won't take them, purchase plastic champagne stoppers from your supplier and tie them down with their wire hood.

Crown caps have a seal on the under side either made of plastic or cork. Not much can go wrong with most plastic lined caps, but cork hardens over time. This means it can't be easily compressed against the bottle lip to make a seal. You don't see cork lined caps that often these days, but should you run into some, you might want to use a few at first to make sure they seal. If you use cork lined caps and find some or all of your bottles failing to carbonate, the caps would be a good bet as a culprit.

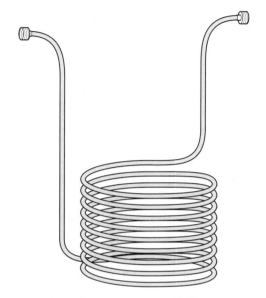

Immersion Wort Chiller

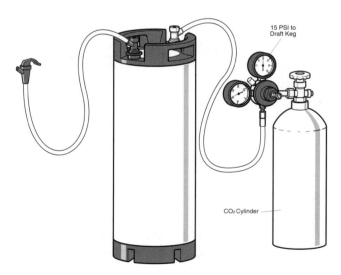

15 PSI to
Draft Keg

CO₂ Cylinder

Draft Beer Tank and Fittings

OPTIONAL EQUIPMENT

In addition to the basics, there are a number of items you will probably want to acquire along the way. They all have a contribution to make relative to ease, precision and quality.

1. A Spare Refrigerator. In some climates, and certainly for classic lagers, this item should be moved from this list to the preceding one, unless you are so fortunate as to have an appropriately cold facility so fermentation and lagering at the required temperatures can be handled some other way. Some brewers cool their fermentations by putting their fermentors inside larger buckets and surrounding them with cold water. In hot climates, you can add ice if necessary. However, a refrigerator makes cooling the fermentation easier and somewhat more exact.

Note that the thermostats of many refrigerators do not allow them to be set quite high enough for the best lager beer fermentation range of 46-50° F. (8-10 C.), but connecting the refrigerator to an "override thermostat" with a sufficient range will solve the problem.

2. A Wort Chiller. The time when wort is being cooled after boiling, and before fermentation begins, is the time during the entire process when beer is most subject to infection. It is, therefore, important to accelerate the cooling process and get the yeast going as quickly as possible.

Probably the easiest and least expensive method is to take the covered boiling kettle, set it in a bathtub filled with cold water, turn on the faucet, and run cold water around it.

The second method is to use a wort chiller. There are a couple of styles which can be bought or built. The easiest to make and use is the "immersion" type which consists of 25-50 feet of copper tube coiled up with brass, male and female, garden hose fittings on the ends. Hoses are attached to run cold water from the nearest source through the coil while it sits in the boiling kettle, and back out to a drain. In this way you can usually add yeast within minutes of the end of the boil. The chiller is sanitized by boiling wort and steam. Don't worry about the inside of the tube, because only water touches that. That's the advantage over the other "counterflow" type.

With the counterflow chiller, the wort is siphoned or pumped through a copper tube. The tube has a larger hose outside it, through which cold water is pumped in the opposite direction. Unfortunately, counterflow chillers are more complicated to build, and with the wort passing through the inside of the tube, this kind of chiller can only be sanitized by intense heat, or by pumping a sanitizing agent through the copper tube to completely remove scale from the wort.

3. A Wine Thief or Bulb-Type Baster. You sometimes need a way to extract samples. One of these will be helpful.

4. A Scale. You'll probably want a scale sooner or later, because such things as hops are very difficult to measure without one. I recommend a small balance scale with a range from at least 1/4 oz. up to 8 oz. in 1/4 oz. increments.

5. pH Papers. If possible, get narrow range plastic-coated papers suitable for testing from around pH 4 to pH 7.

6. Draft Beer Equipment. Should you feel eliminating the work of bottling justifies some cash outlay, you may wish to investigate this option. Should you have access to an actual beer keg, you will need a carbon dioxide cylinder with a pressure guage and faucet, along with all the appropriate fittings.

A much more common approach among home brewers is the use of five gallon, stainless steel, syrup dispensers, the type used for soft drink flavorings. These have handy, "quick disconnect" fittings. Neither type of keg arrangement comes cheap, but this system tends to be a bit less expensive, especially with the current plentiful supply of used tanks. See the discussion of Draft Beer starting on page 104. *Note that the standard, commerical beer keg does not have a pressure relief valve to keep the keg from exploding under excessive pressure. Soda kegs should have a vent on their lids.*

There are also a number of plastic kegs manufactured in Britain, which tend to be more reasonable in price. In addition, several systems have shown up in North America that are patterned on the British system and work in gallon increments. Some do not even require the addition of external CO_2 to drive out the beer. Check with your local supplier, as they are new to the market at the time of this edition.

7. A Bottle Filler. The most common type is a tube that fits into one end of your siphon hose. At the bottom is a valve which opens when pressed onto the bottom of a bottle and closes when the pressure is withdrawn. A filler helps eliminate both messes and oxidation at bottling time. A few layers of folded newspaper under the bottles helps with spills and splashes.

8. A Bottle or Carboy Washer. Similar in principle to the bottle filler, this device attaches to a garden hose or a threaded faucet. It's a wonderful aid in rinsing out bottles and carboys.

9. Mashing and Sparging Equipment. The majority of home brewers will probably always brew using malt extracts and dry malts, rather than relying on grains alone for their fermentables. Most brewers, however, agree that their beers are improved by adding small amounts of grains for an extra freshness of flavor. Sometimes a grain addition is essential to get particular effects.

If using small amounts of grain malts along with your extracts, all you need is a saucepan (2 to 4 quart) to steep the cracked grains in, something to sprinkle or pour hot water with, and a colander to hold the grain and allow the steeping (mashing) water and the rinsing (sparging) water to pass through into the boiling kettle below.

If you go on to all-grain brewing, you will need a somewhat more specialized system, because all of your sugar (and eventually alcohol) will be derived from the grain. Special equipment for this type of brewing is discussed in the section on infusion mashing beginning on page 80.

10. A Grain Mill. If you do go on to work with large amounts of grains, you may well wish to invest in a grain mill.Several types of grain mills are available that can be adjusted to give the coarse grind that you need. You will find models that come with a large hopper more convenient. Many brewers eventually connect them to a 1/2 inch electric drill for convenience.

11. Cheesecloth or Straining Bags. In some situations, you may find cheesecloth or a nylon straining bag useful in straining out either grains, whole or plug hops. Hops or black grains can be tied up in something like this when added to the boil. It helps eliminate the need to strain these ingredients after the boil, saving cleanup work and time.

THE BREWING PROCESS

Place cracked grain in water steep at 150° F. (66 C.)

Strain out cracked grain, collecting runoff in your kettle.

Dissolve dry malt or malt extract in your kettle of hot water.

Stir in any water salts, rice extract or corn sugar (except priming sugar) and bring to a boil.

Tie whole or "plug" hops in a muslin bag. Pellets, may be added loose.

After cooling your wort, rack
to a sterile fermentor
and add yeast.
Attach the lid, filling
the airlock half-full
with water.

Choose a capper from
several different styles.
A 5 gallon batch will bottle
approximately 52
bottles of beer.

Using a bottle filler (shown
here), fill to the level of a
commercial bottle.

Apply even pressure and
capping is quick
and easy.

The hard part is getting a new
batch ready before running out
of the old one.

BASIC PROCEDURES

Your introduction to equipment and ingredients in the sections preceeding this has introduced a lot of terminology that is understandably quite new. You have already begun to see that the "whats", the "whys", and the "hows" of home brewing are hopelessly interrelated.

There is a process, of course, to match up with every ingredient and every piece of equipment. Some processes are self-explanatory. Others should be explained in greater detail. As the following procedures are discussed, you will be led through the various "stages" of brewing, in roughly chronological order. This section will also serve as a ready reference, when you find yourself at the boiling pot, wondering what to do next.

CLEANING

If you're a newcomer to winemaking or brewing, you probably think of cleaning the same way you would if you were washing dishes or canning jars. Boiling water, soaps, and detergents spring immediately to mind. None of these methods, however, should be applied to your brewing equipment or bottles. Boiling can soften plastic, crack crocks, and weaken glass bottles. Soaps and detergents can leave invisible residues, virtually impossible to rinse completely away, which could flavor your beer most unpleasantly, or interfere with its ability to form and hold a head.

Fortunately, when caring for your equipment, you have some better options. It is best to think of cleaning as a process distinct from sanitation.

Cleaning refers primarily to everyday maintainance, the things you do to take care of your equipment after using it. At its simplest level, it involves nothing more than a lot of water.

Anything you have just finished using, and which requires nothing more, is thoroughly rinsed off and allowed to dry. This includes your siphon hose, which can be cleaned by rinsing it off and then forcing water through it with a garden hose. It also includes your bottles. The second part of pouring a beer involves giving the bottle two or three good rinses with water, shaking them to dislodge any residual yeast. If you can, allow your containers to dry upside down.

There are, of course some non-routine cleaning situations. Any veteran home brewer will have encountered supplies of used beer bottles at some point in his career. Bottles are always nice to acquire, but they frequently contain layers of mold, cigarette butts, etc., and need appropriate attention. Fermentation containers may have a resinous, gummy layer midway up the side, where the fermenting beer left its residue. When soaking with water won't do the job, situations like these require extra measures.

Chlorinated TSP (Tri-sodium phosphate) is my choice as a glass cleaner, because it works with either hot or cold water. Use one heaping tablespoon per gallon of water. If you are removing resins from a glass jug, fill the jug with this mixture and let it stand overnight. A quick and easy turn with a brush can then remove the loosened resins. Many bottles will respond to just 10 or 15 minutes in a sink of TSP and hot water. If not, leave the TSP mixture in the bottles and stand them aside for a day or two. After that, a quick brushing out will usually suffice. Rinse at least three times with water.

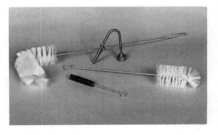

Carboy, Bottle, Fermentation Lock Brushes and Bottle Rinser.

Soda Ash, used at the rate of 1/4 cup per gallon, can also be used for cleaning, but only with hot water. For this reason, don't use it with large glass jugs. Soda Ash is generally somewhat less expensive than TSP. As with TSP, rinse at least three times with clear water.

"B-Brite" is a proprietary product with hydrogen peroxide as the active ingredient. Use an ounce for every one to two gallons of hot water, and let the item to be cleaned soak for 15 to 30 minutes or longer. This product is marvelous for removing stubborn things like "beer stone", the deposit that forms on your boiling kettle after a few uses.

"Straight - A" is another proprietary product with a peroxide base that can clean your equipment . Although, it is a new cleaner to the trade, it's basic recipe has been used in other industries for years. Use 1 tablespoon per gallon of water. Soak bottles and fermentors from five to fifteen minutes. Rinse thoroughly.

SANITATION

It is not enough to make sure that your containers and utensils are clean. Any utensil or container coming in contact with the wort or beer after the boiling of the wort must also be sanitized. The specific goal of sanitation is to eliminate wild yeast and bacteria from any contact with your wort or beer.

One of the most important advances for home brewers in the early 1990's has been the widespread availability of *iodophor (iodine based) sanitizers.* Iodine sanitizers have long been in use in the brewing industry, and it's great that we have access to them as well. Used in reasonable amounts, there is absolutely no way they will give off flavors or aromas to our beers.

Before iodophor, we were forced to use unscented chlorine bleach for effective sanitation, and it usually worked well, but there were some situations in which, when used without rinsing, it could cause problems instead of solving them. Rinsing is always a possibility, of course, but some water supplies, especially wells, are contaminated, so rinsing can undo the sanitation that has just been completed.

To use an iodophor sanitizer, a sink or bucket should be filled with water, and the iodophor mixed in at the rate of one to two tablespoons per five gallons. Follow the instructions for your brand (several are on the market) so your solution will give you titratable iodine of at least 12.5 (and no more than 25) parts per million. Usually, that will mean using at least one tablespoon (and no more than two) per five gallons of water.

After this solution has been thoroughly mixed, it may be used to sanitize anything needing to be treated. Let objects to be sanitized stand in contact with the iodine solution for at least two minutes. Objects sanitized in this way may be used without rinsing, and will not contribute any smell or taste, or anything harmful, to the beer. Recognizing that containers (carboys especially) may be slightly larger than their stated capacity, it's a good practice to use a bit more iodophor than strictly called for to reach the 12.5 parts per million level.

Hoses can be sanitized by siphoning some of the solution between two buckets, and clamping off the flow to let the hose stand full for the required time. Bottles and carboys can be sanitized several days ahead if they can be stored upside down until you're ready to use them. Inverted storage (Make sure case bottoms are clean.) will keep unwanted organisms from falling into your bottles until they're ready to be used.

You may wish to make up an iodine solution and keep it covered and available for incidental use. If so, change the solution every three or four days (or add more iodophor) to retain its full effectiveness. With iodopher, you can see a standing solution lose its strength as the amber color fades. Test strips are also available to test the strength of iodophor solutions.

If sanitizing with *chlorine bleach*, a sink or bucket should be filled with water, and household chlorine bleach mixed in at the rate of two tablespoons per five gallons. After this mixture has been allowed to stand for ten minutes or so, it may be used to sanitize anything needing to be treated. Let objects to be sanitized stand in contact with the chlorine solution for 20-30 minutes and let them drain dry for a minute or two or shake them off. Note that this contact time is much longer than with iodophor.

A solution of this strength will not usually flavor your beer if the sanitized item is still damp when used. If you have problems picking up a bit of chlorine in the flavor of the beer, and must use chlorine, back off a bit on the amount. This may happen if you have a lot of chlorine in your water supply.

Don't shortcut sanitation. If you are sloppy about sanitation, it's a good bet that it will catch up to you sooner or later. Winemakers are sometimes surprised that home brewers take such pains in this area, but beer has significantly less alcohol and acid than wine. Therefore, additional care is needed.

It should be said, however, that it is possible, though less likely, to err in the other direction. I have seen some prospective brewers who were so terrified of contamination possibilities that they were literally afraid to process their beer, or to make beer at all. Less common than a tendency toward sloppiness, unreasoning fear is also a failing. I sometimes think beer, like a growling dog, can sense when it has someone intimidated.

Remember that fermentation is a relatively straightforward process, and beer has been made for a lot longer than we've known anything about yeast or bacteria. Take reasonable care of your sanitation and I think you'll be happy with the results.

British home brewers have traditionally used *bisulfite or metabisulfite solutions* as sanitizing agents. As our North American tradition is directly descended from theirs, many of us followed their lead for years. However, these agents are not as effective against bacteria as either iodophor or chlorine, and they require rinsing which negates the sanitation. The reason "sulfites" are used in Britain is that their household chlorine bleach is perfumed, rendering it useless. Perfumed chlorine bleach has now been introduced in the U.S. as well, and should not be used. As of yet, I have no information indicating that the use of iodophor has reached British hobbyists.

Please note that "sulfite" solutions are used in home winemaking in a number of contexts, and many brewers will have a jug of sulfite around. Never allow these solutions to come in contact with chlorine. Dangerous chlorine gas can be created if that happens.

SIMPLE INFUSION MASHING

Mashing is the cooking process which allows enzymes in the malt to finish converting grain starch to fermentable sugar. This conversion was begun when the grain was malted (sprouted). Though the grain mashing process when beer is being made from scratch can become rather involved, it is not necessary to be too sophisticated when you are using only a pound or two of grain to add some fresh character to a batch of extract beer.

The point, in this case, is not necessarily to extract every last gram of sugar from the grain, but to get some unique character (and sometimes color) into the beer. If your grain is uncracked, crack it in a grain mill, coffee grinder, or a slow-speed blender. Place the cracked grain in a pot and cover it with enough water to float the grain. Cover the pot and set it in the oven with the thermostat set at 150° F. (65 C.) and leave it there for 45 minutes to an hour. You can do this on the stove top as well, but you'll have to watch the temperature a bit more closely.

It will probably not be necessary with small amounts of grain malts, but should you go into all-grain brewing, or to the point where you're relying on a lot of grain in your batch, you will probably want to test your mash to see if all the starch has been converted. This is done as follows. Take a few drops of liquid from the mash, placing it in a white saucer or plate. Take care not to pick up any pieces of the grain husk as you do so. Add a drop or two of your iodophor sanitizer to the liquid, and mix it in. If the liquid turns dark blue or black, starch is still present and the mashing must continue. If the iodine blends with it, essentially becoming colorless, all the starch has been converted and the mash can be stopped at any time. Don't allow your mash to go on longer than an hour and a half, however. There won't be much, if any, enzyme activity left at that point, and you may begin to extract undesirable elements from the grain.

After mashing, the grain must be sparged or rinsed. Remove it from the oven and pour the mash water into your boiling pot through a strainer or colander. Pour hot water through the grain, rinsing (sparging) the grain as thoroughly as possible until the runoff is clear. Ideally, the sparging water should be between 150 and 165° F. (66 to 74 C.) though hot tap water will suffice. Then discard the spent grain and procede to boil the wort as you normally would. All of the lighter grain malts up through crystal malt should be mashed.

Sparging the Grain.

Koji (Aspergillus Oryzae) is an enzyme that converts grain starch to fermentable sugar. It is traditionally used in the conversion of rice for sake, but it can be very useful with barley malts as well. It may be added during the mash if you are using grain you aren't sure of. Take a cup or two of water and stir in about half a tablespoon of Koji for each pound of grain used (1 Tbl. per Kilo). Hold the temperature of the entire mash at 130° F. (54 C.) for 10 minutes before proceding to raise the temperature further.

The complex of enzymes contained in malt grains themselves, which effects the conversion of starches into fermentable sugars, is commonly known as "Diastase" or "Amylase." You may purchase this separately as well, and add it in the same manner as Koji. Half a teaspoon per pound of grain should suffice.

BOILING

You will have seen in the earlier section of *Procedures For Ales and Stouts*, that boiling is the stage of beermaking where all the ingredients, (except the yeast and priming sugar) come together. Your boiling pot will ideally hold up to five gallons, leaving room for the foaming that occurs during the boil. If not, you can preboil some water, cooling it and adding it at the end of the main boil, or split the batch into two smaller pots.

Boiling of the malt with the hops, and any additional adjuncts and water treatments takes 60 to 90 minutes. The boil will also sanitize the ingredients, and it will solubilize hop alpha acids to bitter the wort. In addition, proteins that contribute to a cloudy appearance in finished beer, will largely be removed by the heat and turbulance of the boil.

Most people want to know if they should put the lid on the pot to cut down evaporation. Since you can always boil and cool some extra water to cover this loss, and since an uncovered boil helps get rid of some unpleasant, volotile components, it is more important to use the lid only as a means to getting a strong, rolling boil, and then remove it . If necessary, cover the pot part way, but be very careful that it does not lodge down tight and promote a boilover!

The final stage of boiling is cooling. You can move the pot to a large tub of water, circulating plenty of cool water around the covered pot until the temperature drops to 85° to 90° F. (32 C.).

Should you have a wort chiller, cooling the wort is acheived more quickly. Follow the instructions with your style of chiller. Should you wish to take a sample of your beer to measure it's specific gravity, do so after it is cooled and topped back to a full five gallons. Record your reading and test again at the end of fermentation if you wish to calculate your alcohol content.

FERMENTATION

This is the stage where the highly sweet, and somewhat bitter, wort you have just finished boiling is activated by the yeast to froth and foam; and seemingly by magic, become beer.

After cooling the wort, it is transferred, by pouring into a plastic bucket or preferably by siphoning into one or two glass carboys, filled to below the shoulder, and fitted with the appropriate lids and fermentation locks. Always allow at least a gallon of head space above the liquid for the foam that will rise during active fermentation. If you are shy of the full five gallons, boil some additional water and cover and cool it, adding it as soon as practical. Aeration at this stage will help the yeast grow and start to work quickly.

Add your yeast and attatch your fermentation lock, making sure it is filled with sanitary water, half full, or it won't work as a one-way valve to release a buildup of CO_2 . Often in a matter of hours, you will see the yeast begin rising to the surface, followed by the formation of a head of foam. If you used the proper amount of yeast, your fermentation should be complete within a week in warm conditions (63° to 75° F) common to fermenting ales.

The fermentation temperature for lagers is generally colder than for ales (45° to 60° F) and can take up to three weeks to reach completion, especially under controlled refrigeration temperatures. The lower temperature combined with the differences in yeast strains, decreases the production of the stronger esters (fruity aromatics like bananas and apples) found in ales. At the end of fermentation, transfer the beer to a sanitized jug, topped full with sanitized water and closed with a fermentation lock or stopper, and begin lagering (See the next section).

When the visible signs of fermentation are over, take a sample for a specific gravity reading and for tasting. It should taste like relatively dry, flat beer, and be reasonably close to the expected final gravity. Siphon away from the sediment on the bottom, into a sanitized container, prime with sugar, and bottle. (See Carbonation, pp. 67-69 for more details on bottling.)

Alternatively, allow the beer to ferment in the first container until the foam drops back to the surface, transfer by siphoning the beer to a second container, preferably a glass five gallon carboy. Avoid splashing at this stage. Fill the jug into the neck with additional, boiled and cooled water, if necessary, and attatch a fermentation lock. Let the jug stand three or four days to allow further settling, and then siphon the beer to a sanitized bottling bucket, prime and bottle.

Personally, I prefer the second method, because moving the beer off the settlings an extra time seems to provide a cleaner bottling, with less sediment left behind in the bottom of my bottles. The trade-off is that the first method involves one less processing of the beer.

LAGERING

A traditional style lager beer should be aged after fermentation for a period of at least three weeks. At a brewery, this would normally be done in bulk, at about 32 ° F. (0 C.). Lager beers take their name from this cold aging (lagering) process. During this time, a subtle change takes place in the beer as it gains smoothness and delicacy. This is in contrast to the more rough and ready ales and stouts, which may be consumed as soon as full, or sometimes even partial, carbonation has been achieved and the yeast has begun to drop to the bottom of the bottle. For all-grain brewers, lagering also helps precipitate the protein which causes "chill hazes", a phenomenon in which perfectly clear beers become cloudy when served from a cold refrigerator.

Obviously, you have to have a spare refrigerator if you're going to lager your beers in bulk. *Do not attempt it at warmer temperatures that will encourage bacterial growth.* Unless you have refrigeration capacity, age your beer in the bottle, where the carbon dioxide will afford it some additional protection.

If you've been lagering for a number of weeks, you may wish to add a pack of yeast at bottling time along with your priming sugar (in case your original yeast is no longer active). However, if the beer has been lagering for less than six weeks, simply drag the end of your racking tube for three or four inches across the bottom of the lagering tank just as you begin siphoning. That should stir up enough live yeast cells so that they get sucked up with the beer, and will be present to help carbonate it.

CARBONATION

Most home brewed beers are carbonated by the time-honored method known as "bottle conditioning", in which a limited amount of fermentation is allowed to take place in the bottle. The objective of this fermentation is to produce and trap carbon dioxide, though there is a very slight increase in alcohol content.

Old-time, prohibition era, home brewers used to quickly bottle their still fermenting beer when the specific gravity dropped to the appropriate level. Unfortunately, this can be a bit tricky unless you are quite experienced, and the desired point can be reached as easily at three a.m. as at any other time. Therefore, such varied results as flat beer, late night bottling sessions, or blown bottles and sticky messes, were relatively common. In fact, to this day, the exploding bottle remains probably the most widespread and enduring bit of American home brewing folklore. Such problems can, of course, be quite discouraging, not only to brewers themselves, but to those who share their households as well. Happily, they are easily avoided.

The simplest method of carbonating home brewed beer is to let the beer ferment completely out. Once the beer is flat, you can then "prime" it with a measured amount of sugar to give you just the right amount of carbonation. If your beer is being bottled within a few days after the end of fermentation, you should use approximately 3/4 cup Corn Sugar to five gallons of beer. If your brew has been lagered, it will have had time to vent some additional trapped carbon dioxide left over from fermentation, and you may wish to increase the priming sugar to a full cup.

The best way to add priming sugar is to stir it into 1 to 2 cups of water. Heat to boiling, stirring occasionally, and boil for five minutes. Boiling turns the mixture into a syrup which will dissolve easily in the beer. Ascorbic Acid may be added to it as well. Siphon the beer off of its sediment into an appropriate container, add the sugar syrup, stir thoroughly, siphon the beer immediately into bottles, and cap them. Store the cases at cellar temperature(not refrigerated) until the beer is fully primed.

Should you taste a beer you're about to bottle and decide it needs some extra hop flavor and aroma, you may make a correction with an alternate priming method. Tie 1/4 to 1/2 oz. of your freshest whole hops in cheesecloth and put them in 2 cups of water and boil from two to five minutes. Remove the hops, add your priming sugar, heat once again to boiling, and procede as you normally would.

After you've gained some experience, you may wish to try the traditional priming method known as kraeusening, assuming the name hasn't scared you off. It simply means priming a finished beer by adding to it an amount of a new wort which has just begun to ferment. Add enough wort to raise the gravity by 4 to 5 points. That should give you 3 to 4 points of gravity to ferment.

Whichever priming method you use, your ales should be given 1 to 2 weeks in the bottle at cellar temperature. As clarity is generally considered more important for lagers, they should have 3 to 4 weeks minimum. Store your beer upright in the cases, away from light and at room temperature until full carbonation is obtained. You may refrigerate the beer after it is carbonated, to help maintain it's fresh hop and malt characteristics.

FINAL GRAVITIES

The higher the malt content of a given beer, the higher the final gravity will be. If you had a wort that had a four to five malt to sugar ratio like many old-time homebrews, it would ferment all the way down to approximately zero (1.000). As the ratio of malt to sugar is increased, the final gravity you may expect also goes up in relatively direct proportion until, with an all malt wort, it reaches a point which is roughly one-fourth the starting gravity of the wort. Thus you may calculate the expected final gravity of most all malt worts by dividing the starting gravity by four.

All this may seem frighteningly complex, but it really isn't if you remember that your saccharometer doesn't measure sugar directly, but infers it by indicating the weight of a solution. In introducing the saccharometer, it was mentioned that sugar is heavier than water, but alcohol is lighter. Therefore, if you were able to ferment a solution of pure, highly refined sugar, the gravity would start out above 1.000 and finish below it, around .990.

Malt, however, is not so highly refined, and contains additional elements which provide body (and weight). Thus, more malt means more weight and a higher final gravity, but more alcohol derived from a refined sugar means the final gravity will be lower.

This should explain why beers with a higher sugar content should finish closer to zero, while high malt beers terminate somewhat higher. By derivation, you should be able to see why you need to raise the gravity slightly more than the actual sugar content desired when kraeusening with high malt worts.

Note that a very black beer will probably finish a bit higher still. The reason a black grain, such as black patent malt will do this is that most of the fermentables were burned out of it when it was kilned. It can still add other elements to a wort, increasing the percentage of non-fermentables, and thereby raising the final gravity. In most cases, dividing the starting gravity by three will establish the upper limit of the final gravity range for these beers, though some stouts can go a bit higher. This will also be true, of course, for beers with a high dextrin content, either because of a high mash temperature (in the case of all-grain beers) or because powdered dextrin has been added.

Obviously, if using the final gravity as a benchmark to bottle your beer, you should also look at your beer for the absence of visible signs of fermentation, and also taste the beer to see if any obvious sweetness remains.

SERVING

I can't tell you the optimum temperature at which to serve your beer, because that's something you have to decide. I will say, though, that over the years I've personally come to prefer my ales, porters, and stouts between 55 and 60° F. (13-16 C.), and my lagers between 45 and 50° F. (7-10 C.).

All bottle conditioned beers have a tiny bit of sediment at the bottom of the bottle. There may be some who regard this as a minor annoyance, but I find it part of the beer's charm, a reminder of its natural origin. In any case, sediment is not particularly pleasant to taste, so your beer should be poured slowly into a tilted glass until the sediment approaches the lip of the bottle. Then tip the bottle upright again, not allowing any sediment to pass. As a skilled hand will waste very few drops of beer in the process, rigorous practice is suggested.

OXIDATION: A CAUTIONARY TALE

Whenever your beer is being moved from one container to another, at any stage in the beermaking process after fermentation begins, you should take pains to expose it to as little oxygen as possible. This means making sure that splashing is minimized by having the hose go right to the bottom of the container you're filling. It also means making sure that settling and lagering containers are filled so that the air surface is kept to a minimum, and that your beer is stored as cool as possible.

Careless exposure of your beer to the air can severely affect the quality. Splashing is only desirable after your wort has cooled, and before it has begun to ferment. A reasonable amount of oxygen at that stage is beneficial to yeast growth and should have no harmful effects. That is most definitely not the case later on.

FORMULATING YOUR OWN RECIPES

This is not particularly difficult, and you'll undoubtedly want to give it a try. As a general guideline, I would suggest an absolute minimum of 3 lbs. of malt extract (or dry malt) and a maximum of 1 1/2 lbs. of corn sugar or other adjuncts in a five gallon batch. Grains may be varied at will in the course of experimentation and creativity. This is the sort of thing that helps make brewing fun.

Hops, of course, may be increased or decreased according to taste. You may also change varieties, or blend a number of types, to achieve particular effects. The subject of hops can be complex. The amount of alpha (lupulic) and beta (lupulinic) acids present determines the potential bitterness in any given hop with alpha acids accounting for most of it. Consequently, the bitterness of a hop is normally rated in terms of the alpha acid content. The amount of essential oils determines the degree of aromatics. The variety you use determines the flavor and aroma you will get.

Also, brewers are often stunned to realize how much it can change a recipe to make the beer with different strains of yeast. Some strains are so different from each other that, if you split a batch, you may have trouble believing the two halves are actually the same beer.

Congratulate yourself for getting the rudiments of brewing under your belt. Hopefully by now you've brewed an ale (or at least have your calendar marked for your first brewing session.) The section on lagers that follows is very similar to the ale section in that the recipes will look familiar, refer to Fermentation (p. 65) if you need a refresher on the different in fermentation methods.

Hopefully you will move on to the advanced sections that follow, if not immediately, as soon as you have become acquainted with the ingredients and techniques already introduced.

PROCEDURES FOR LAGERS

The procedure for these beers differs in some respects from the procedure for ales and stouts. In general, it is a slightly more sophisticated approach to brewing. If you really love a good pilsner, however, by all means try your hand.

Perhaps you will go all the way, with cold fermentation followed by a period of lagering (See Lagering pp. 66-67), only for particular showpiece beers. The rest of the time, cool fermentation, followed by aging in the bottles at cellar temperatures, will be employed. Good beers may be made by either method, though most lager beers can be improved with the full treatment.

COOKING

Start by reading your recipe to see if you will be using any grain malts. If so, start at point "A." If not, skip to point "B."

A. If your recipe calls for one or more grain malts (or other grains), place the cracked or ground grain in a kitchen pan, cover with water, heat to approximately 150° F (66 C.), cover and let stand (either on the stove top or in the oven) for 45 minutes to an hour before you're actually ready to start to work.

Place a colander over your boiling kettle and pour in the grain. Rinse through the grain with hot water, at least 130° F. (54 C.) but no hotter than 170° F. (77 C.), letting the steeping water and rinse water collect in the pot below, until a clear runoff is obtained. Discard the grain. The liquid collected becomes part of the boil. If unable to fit all the grain into your colander at once, divide it up, and rinse it in stages. Proceed to step B.

B. Thoroughly dissolve any of the following called for in your recipe: Malt Extract, Dry Malt, any Sugar *except* priming sugar, Rice Extract, Dextrin Powder, Gypsum, Salt, Chalk, Epsom Salts, Irish Moss, or Yeast Nutrient, in two or more gallons of water (as much as possible). Heat to a rolling boil. Stir in half of the Bittering Hops and boil for 30 minutes, stirring occasionally. Add the rest of the Bittering Hops and boil for 30 more minutes, adding the Aromatic Hops during the last two minutes.

At the end of the boil, the wort should be cooled as quickly as possible to a temperature between 70 and 80° F. (21-27 C.), so the yeast can be added.

FERMENTATION

Siphon your cooled wort into one or more sanitized glass jugs, filling them no more than two thirds full. Add Yeast, attach a fermentation lock to each, and allow fermentation to proceed.

Fermentation for lager beers is essentially the same as for ales except the temperature should be kept colder and lager yeast is used. With dried lager yeasts, the ideal temperature is between 50 and 55° F. (10 to 15 C.), though some commercial cultures (available in liquid form) can ferment down as low as 40 ° F. (5 C.). If enough yeast is used and sanitation procedures are carefully followed, fermentation will normally be concluded in about 10 days to two weeks.

When apparent yeast activity has ceased, and the saccharometer reading is somewhere near the anticipated final gravity; taste the sample you're testing to see if it tastes like dry, flat beer. Go on to lagering the beer as the next step.

LAGERING

True lager beers must, logically enough, be lagered. When fermentation has finished, siphon your beer into a second glass jug, topping it up with previously boiled and cooled water.

Stopper up the jug and store the beer under refrigeration as close to 32 degrees F. (0 C.) as possible for at least three weeks. You might lager your beer for as long as three months, but you'll probably find the space in your refrigerator is more profitably used for lagering subsequent batches. Temperature is important, so don't try lagering unless you can at least get it down to 40 degrees F. (4 C.). Without that sort of control, you should bottle your beer at the end of fermentation, and age it in the bottles.

BOTTLING

When lagering is finished, siphon the beer away from the sediment. If necessary, stir in half a pack of lager yeast along with your priming sugar syrup (see p. 68), siphon the beer into bottles and cap them. After a week or two, chill a bottle and try it. If enough yeast has dropped out so that the beer is clear, it is ready to drink. When that happens, immediately chill a couple more to sip while cooking up a new batch. This rigorously disciplined approach to home brewing will help maintain the proper level of inspiration, allowing you to get the most possible enjoyment from your chosen craft.

Rigorous practice assures success.

Lager Beer Recipes

AMERICAN STYLE LAGER - 5 U.S. GAL. (19 LITERS)

3 lbs. (1.4 kilos) Light Dry Malt
1 lb. (454 grams) Rice Extract *or* Corn Sugar
1/4 tsp. Gypsum
1/4 tsp. Salt
3/4 oz. (21 grams) Bittering Hops (Spalt, Cluster, *or* Hallertau)
1/4 oz. (7 grams) Aromatic Hops (Hallertau *or* Cascade)
Water to 5 gallons (19 liters)
3/4 to 1 cup Corn Sugar for priming
1/2 oz. (14 grams) Lager Yeast

> Starting S.G. 1.036 - Final S.G. 1.006-8
> Alcohol by vol. 3 1/2% - Suggested IBU 10-13

NORTH EUROPEAN STYLE PILS - 5 U.S. GAL. (19 LITERS)

4 lbs. (1.8 kilos) Light Dry Malt
1 lb. (454 grams) Lager Malt
4 oz. (113 grams) Munich Malt (Munich 10)
1/4 tsp. Gypsum
1/4 tsp. Salt
1 3/4 oz. (50 grams) Bittering Hops (Hallertau *or* Liberty)
1/2 oz. (14 grams) Aromatic Hops (Hallertau *or* Mt. Hood)
Water to 5 gallons (19 liters)
3/4 to 1 cup Corn Sugar for priming
1/2 oz. (14 grams) Lager Yeast

> Starting S.G. 1.044 - Final S.G.1.011
> Alcohol by vol. 4% - Suggested IBU 25-27

CZECH STYLE PILSNER - 5 U.S. GAL. (19 LITERS)

4 1/2 lbs. (2 kilos) Light Dry Malt
1 1/2 lbs. (680 grams) Munich Malt (Munich 10)
8 oz. (227 grams) Wheat Malt
2 oz. (57 grams) Black Patent Malt
2 oz. (57 grams) 100% Dextrin Powder (optional)
2 1/2 oz. (71 grams) Bittering Hops (Saaz)
1/4 (7 grams) Aromatic Hops (Saaz)
Water to 5 gallons (19 liters)
3/4 to 1 cup Corn Sugar for priming
1/2 oz. (14 grams) Lager Yeast

> Starting S.G. 1.050 - Final S.G. 1.012-13
> Alcohol by vol. 4 3/4% - Suggested IBU 30-40

VIENNA STYLE AMBER LAGER - 5 U.S. GAL. (19 LITERS)

4 1/2 lbs. (2 kilos) Amber Dry Malt
2 lbs. (907 grams) Vienna Malt (4)
or 8 oz. (227 grams) Caravienne Malt (20)
2 oz. (57 grams) 100% Dextrin Powder (optional)
1/4 tsp. Gypsum
1/8 tsp. Salt
1/2 tsp. Powdered Chalk
1 oz. (28 grams) Bittering Hops (Hallertau *or* Tettnang)
Water to 5 gallons (19 liters)
3/4 to 1 cup Corn Sugar for priming
1/2 oz. (14 grams) Lager Yeast

> Starting S.G. 1.047-48 - Final S.G. 1.012-13
> Alcohol by vol. 4 1/4% - Suggested IBU 20-24

MUNICH STYLE DARK - 5 U.S. GAL. (19 LITERS)

4 lbs. (1.8 kilos) Light Dry Malt
8 oz. (227 grams) Munich Malt (Munich 10)
8 oz. (227 grams) Munich Malt (Munich 20)
8 oz. (227 grams) Crystal Malt (Caramel 60)
4 oz. (113 grams) Black Malt
2 oz. (57 grams) 100% Dextrin Powder
1/4 tsp. Gypsum
1/8 tsp. Salt
1/2 tsp. Powdered Chalk
1 1/2 oz. (43 grams) Bittering Hops (Hallertau *or* Spalt)
Water to 5 gallons (19 liters)
3/4 to 1 cup Corn Sugar for priming
1/2 oz. (14 grams) Lager Yeast

> Starting S.G. 1.050 - Final S.G. 1.015
> Alcohol by vol. 4 1/4% - Suggested IBU 18-24

BOCK - 5 U.S. GAL. (19 LITERS)

3 1/2 lbs. (1.6 kilos) Amber Malt Extract
2 lbs. (907 grams) Light Dry Malt
4 oz. (113 grams) Munich Malt (Munich 20)
4 oz. (113 grams) Crystal Malt (Caramel 40)
8 oz. (227 grams) Chocolate Malt
4 oz. (113 grams) 100% Dextrin Powder
1/2 tsp. Gypsum
1/2 tsp. Salt
1/2 tsp. Powdered Chalk
1 1/2 oz. (43 grams)Bittering Hops (Tettnang)
1/2 oz. (14 grams) Aromatic Hops (Liberty *or* Tettnang)
Water to 5 gallons (19 liters)
3/4 cup Corn Sugar for priming
1/2 oz. (14 grams) Lager Yeast

> Starting S.G. 1.055 -   Final S.G. 1.015
> Alcohol by vol. 5% - Suggested IBU 20-26

DOPPELBOCK - 5 U.S. GAL. (19 LITERS)

6 1/2 lbs. (3 kilos) to 7 lbs. (3.2 kilos) Light Malt Extract
2 lbs. (907 grams) Amber Malt Extract
2 lbs. (907 grams) Munich Malt (Munich 10)
1 1/2 lbs. (681 grams) Crystal Malt (Caramel 40)
6 oz. (170 grams) Chocolate Malt
2 oz. (57 grams) Black Patent Malt
8 oz. (227 grams) 100% Dextrin Powder
or 4 oz. (113 grams) Lactose
1/2 tsp. Gypsum
1/2 tsp. Salt
1/2 tsp. Powdered Chalk
1 3/4 oz. (50 grams) Bittering Hops (Eroica)
1 oz. (28 grams) Aromatic Hops (Cascade *or* Hallertau)
Water to 5 gallons (19 liters)
3/4 cup Corn Sugar for priming
1/2 oz. (14 grams) Lager Yeast

Starting S.G. 1.072 -   Final S.G. 1.025
Alcohol by vol. 5% - Suggested IBU 24-30

PROCEDURES FOR ADVANCED BREWING

All right, so now you've brewed a few batches, and by now you've learned that the basics of brewing good beer are not that hard to grasp, so you're ready to move on to some areas requiring a bit more sophistication.

Here are a few refinements you don't need to master as a beginning brewer, but which will increase your enjoyment of the hobby once you look into them.We start with an introduction to all- grain brewing.

BREWING FROM GRAIN

If you suggest all-grain mashing to extract brewers, they will often respond that they could never try anything that complicated. But thinking this way, a lot of folks sell themselves short. You don't start extract brewing knowing all there is to know about brewing, and you don't have to start out knowing all the nuances of mashing either.

The fact is that these days there's plenty of information available about brewing from grain. You will probably find that brewing from scratch is more fun than having things done for you. It takes a bit longer, but it's a far more interesting process, and it saves money too.

There's no question that grain brewing, once you've gained some experience, will increase your personal satisfaction with brewing. At that point, you won't just be a homebrewer any more. You'll be on your way to becoming a true brewmaster.

1. Infusion Mashing What follows is designed to take you through the process of infusion mashing. Infusion is the easiest of the three mashing methods for beginners to work with, and with modern malts, it's adaptable for virtually any kind of beer. Upward Infusion and Decoction (the other two methods) will be discussed later as variations.

While it is true that a few people with a good technical background are able to bypass extract brewing entirely, moving directly to grain, most people like to get at least a few batches under their belts before moving up. In any case, I presume that, as a potential grain brewer, you are already brewing with malt extracts, augmented by modest amounts of grain, or that, at least, you will have thoroughly read the first part of this book to acquire a sound background in basic brewing techniques.

What Equipment Is Needed.

You will need the following items:

1. Two stainless or enamel boiling kettles. One will be your "mash tun" and should have at least a 4 gallon capacity, and the other will hold your sparge water, or "liquor," and later double as the boiling kettle, at least 8 gallons.

2. A large, heavy duty, stirring spoon or paddle.

3. A colander or large strainer.

4. A lauter tun or sparger. This consists of a 5 to 7 gallon plastic bucket with a plastic drum tap affixed. This is either lined with a large nylon straining bag held in place by the lock lid of the bucket, or a second bucket with a lot of holes drilled in its base is nested inside the first bucket. In either case, the straining bag or bucket with holes will hold back the grain during the rinsing process that follows the mash. If possible, also run a vinyl hose from the drum tap to the bottom of the container where you'll be collecting the runoff. The straining bag should be large enough to fill the bucket all the way to the edges when the mash is poured in.

5. A metal probe thermometer.

6. A saucepan or other container used to scoop hot water from the large kettle, and pour it slowly through the colander.

7. *A stove or propane burner* capable of heating at least six and a half gallons of liquid to a rolling boil.

The only tricky thing about working from grain is that your yield will vary a bit, not only because of what you do, and the materials you use, but based also on the efficiency of your particular mashing and sparging equipment.

In practice, this usually means that a new grain brewer may get a lower specific gravity than he or she was expecting, or than a given recipe indicates. A good precaution is to have a bag of light dried malt powder on hand. Then, if necesary, you can add enough dry malt sugar to raise the gravity up to your goal. Don't be embarrased about doing this. All new grain brewers, including me, have gone through it. It doesn't mean you've messed up the mashing process. It just means you'll have to learn how efficient your equipment and techniques are during your first few batches, and that will soon tell you whether more malt is needed to target your gravity.

Estimating Your Batch.

Doing a little quick figuring on your calculator or adding machine will make the recipe design easier. I'm not going to incorporate metric equivilents into the discussion that follows (except for temperatures), because the text contains quite a few numbers as it is, and I don't want to confuse people. If you feel it necessary to work in metric weights and measures, you may make the conversion by following the information on page 112.

How Much Water To Use.

The standard ratio of water to grain is 1.1 quarts of water for every pound of grain. Commonly, I like to express this as 2.75 gallons of water per 10 pounds of grain. That's easy for a lot of recipes, except that many recipes won't call for exactly 10 lbs. of grain, so you may need to make a minor adjustment.

Let's say, for example, that your recipe calls for 9 lbs. That is 9/10 (or .9) of 10, so all you have to do is multiply 2.75 x .9 = 2.48, which tells you that 2 1/2 gallons of water in your mash should be close enough.

If your recipe calls for 8 1/2 lbs., simply multiply 2.75 x .85 instead of .9, and your answer will be 2.34 gallons. A recipe calling for 11 lbs. of grain would call for 2.75 to be multiplied by 1.1, and give you an answer of 3.03 gallons, etc.

Once you've figured out how much water is required for your mash, the only other calculation needed, unless you're formulating your own recipe, is to make sure the mash you're planning will fit in the mash tun you intend to use.

What Volume of Kettle Space Will Be Needed.

To do this, you simply add two figures. The first you already know. That's the number of gallons of water in the mash. Let's say we're doing that first recipe we've just been figuring out, the one with nine lbs. of grain. As was just demonstrated, your mash will have **2.48** gallons of water.

Now, you need to do a short calculation to figure out how much space your grain will take up once it has been added. *Figure .08 gallons volume for every pound of grain.* In other words, the calculation will read as follows: .08 **x 9 = .72 gallons.** Then you add this figure to the amount of water: **2.48 + .72 = 3.20** gallons, which shows that you will have no trouble conducting this mash in a four gallon pot.

The easiest thing of all to figure is the volume of sparge water. *That's equal to the final volume of beer.* Since we're talking about a five gallon batch, you should put five gallons of water, or slightly more, into your eight gallon kettle.

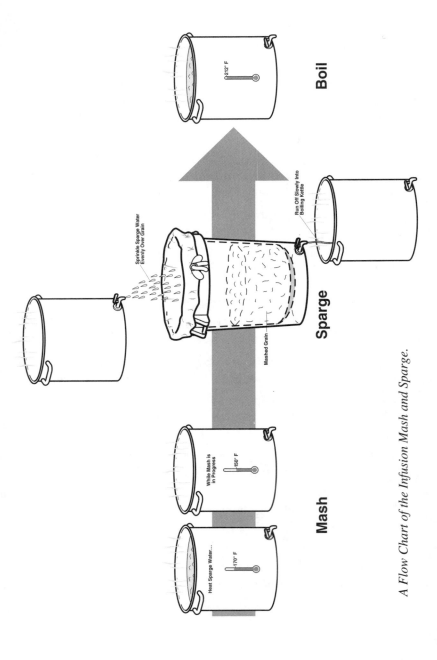

Mash

Sparge

Boil

Heat Sparge Water...

170° F

While Mash is in Progress

150° F

Sprinkle Sparge Water Evenly Over Grain

Mashed Grain

Run Off Slowly Into Boiling Kettle

212° F

A Flow Chart of the Infusion Mash and Sparge.

The Mash Itself.

First begin heating both your mash and sparge water. After you've done two or three batches, you'll probably learn to time the heating of the sparge water, and have a better idea when to start so it will be hot by the time it is needed. At first, however, just make sure to allow enough time. You can always turn it off for awhile if it gets hot too soon. You will ultimately use your sparge water at approximately 170° F (77 C.).

Depending on the relative power of your heat sources, you might start heating both kettles simultaneously, but it's the mash water you're immediately concerned with. As quickly as possible, heat the mash water to 10° F. above the temperature you wish the mash to be, once the grain is stirred in, so the water will be somewhere between 160 and 168° F. (71-76 C.) When your water is hot enough, turn off the heat, and carefully stir in the cracked grain, being careful to break up any "balls" of grain that form.

When the grain has been stirred in thoroughly, take the temperature. If it needs to be raised, turn the heat back on, and make the adjustment, stirring thoroughly, and taking temperature readings until the desired level has been reached. If the temperature needs to be lowered, do so by thoroughly stirring in a little cold water until the temperature is where you want it. You have about 10 minutes to make any "fine tuning" adjustments desired without appreciably affecting the character of the wort.

Once this has been done, you have begun the mashing step known as the "sugar rest." In infusion mashing the sugar rest is very nearly the entire process. The grain is steeped at temperatures usually between 145 and 158° F (63-70 C). During the first 30 minutes or so of the rest, enzymes contained in the barley malt convert the starch in the grain to fermentable sugars and dextrins.

To understand what's happening, think of grain starches as large, very complex, molecules, too large and complex, in fact, for yeast to readily digest. During mashing, two groups of enzymes operate on starch: sugar producing enzymes and dextrin producing enzymes.

The function of the sugar producing enzymes is to break up those molecules into smaller, simpler units the yeast will be able to work with during fermentation, converting them once more into alcohol and carbon dioxide. These simple units are called "fermentable sugars." The enzymes which convert starches all the way to fermentable sugars become active as soon as the temperature reaches 125° F. (52 C.) or so, and their activity is most intense between 140 and 149° F. (60-65 C).

Dextrin producing enzymes have a similar function, but they don't do as complete a starch conversion. The complex starch molecules are converted to an intermediate form halfway between starch and sugar, not as complex as starch, but not simple enough for yeast to readily work with. Dextrins, therefore, contribute "full mouth feel" and a touch of sweetness to a beer, rather than alcohol. The dextrin producing enzymes are most active between 150 and 158° F (66-70 C.) Although it is true that yeasts may break down dextrins over an extended period of time, dextrins should generally be considered unfermentable for most practical purposes.

What all this means is that you can change your beer just by changing the temperature of the mash. A beer made from a 155-158° F. (68-70 C) mash will have a fuller mouthfeel, with slightly more sweetness and less alcohol, than an identical beer mashed at 148° F. (64 C), because the dextrin producing enzymes are within their maximum range of efficiency, while the sugar producing enzymes are not. The reverse effect might be achieved by mashing between 140 and 145° F. (60-63 C), which would get maximum efficiency from your sugar producing enzymes, and much less from the dextrin producers. In fact, subtle variations will take place with every degree of variation in mash temperature, which gives the careful brewer a tremendous amount of control.

Ultimately, the control a brewer enjoys is the most compelling thing about grain brewing. That's what makes it worth spending the extra time necessary to work with grain, even though lots of good beers are made using malt extracts. If spending twice as long brewing up your batches bothers you, start collecting the containers to do 10 gallon batches instead of five, so you get twice the amount of beer for your trouble.

I mentioned earlier that the time during mashing when the enzyme activity takes place is during the first 30 minutes of the sugar rest. A sugar rest, however, will normally run at least an hour, and most commonly, 90 minutes. What happens after the enzyme activity finishes is that you're essentially making tea, and just as in tea making, the longer the mash steeps, the more color and flavor you will extract. You can stop the sugar rest and move on as soon as your desired color and flavor have been reached. *Note that with sugar rests longer than 90 minutes (as suggested in some of the older literature), there is increased potential for extracting undesirable elements.*

At the end of the sugar rest, comes a step called "mashing off," in which the mash temperature is raised to 170°F. (77 C) prior to sparging. Apply heat, and gently stir your mash until your mash off tempertaure is reached. Scoop out 2 quarts of your sparge water and place it at the bottom of your lauter tun, this is a good time to check that you have shut off the drain valve on the tun. The water that you add to the bucket is called "foundation water." It preheats the

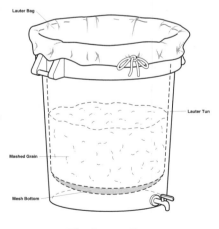

The Lauter Tun.

tun and helps to cushion and float the grain, keeping them from compacting, which would reduce your yield of sugar.

Mashing-off is often misunderstood. The primary purpose is to increase your yield by getting the temperature up so the sugars can flow more efficiently from the grain. The principle is the same as that of molasses flowing more freely in July than in January, though the temperature range is different. With this in mind, beginners should get the temperature as close to 170° F. as possible, or even slightly higher, when mashing off, recognizing that some degrees will be lost in the transfer to the "lauter tun."

Transfer all the mash into the bucket, with the fitted nylon straining bag held in place, just off the bottom, with the lid snap-locked around the rim. The lid can be cut in a few odd places along the side to allow room for the bag and still lock into place. You will need to have a hollow area in the lid, just use a pocket knife to cut away the middle. This will allow you to set a colander or sieve in the hollow.

The Sparge.

"Sparging" is simply the process of rinsing all the "goodies" out of the grain so they can be collected in your boiling kettle. When the mash has been placed in the "lauter tun" (sparging container), clean out your mashing kettle so you can use it to collect the "sweet wort." It's ok to leave the mash alone for 10 or 15 minutes, to allow some settling to occur. The main trick in sparging is adding the 170° F. (77 C) sparge water gently to the top of the mash in such a way that it doesn't dig holes in the grain bed. Digging holes might allow the sparge water to bypass some of the sugar in the upper grain, and lower your yield. A colander will spread the water being poured into it, forming a reasonably gentle spray. Alternatively, a commercial sparging bucket is now being marketed and carried by many homebrew supply shops. It comes complete with a rotating spray arm to accomplish a very gentle sparging of the grain.

Open the bottom valve on the sparger so the "sweet wort" begins to drain slowly at the same rate you are adding sparge water to the top. The trick is to keep the surface of the water 1-2 inches above the surface of the grain until all the water runs out. Keep the sparge water hot the whole time, or your yield could be reduced. Ideally, the sparging process should take about an hour, though you may find it difficult to keep it going more than 45 minutes with small batches.

One simple refinement to this system is to drain and collect some of the first runoff into a small container, and then gently spread it back over the surface of the grain bed before beginning the actual sparge. You may recirculate two to four quarts of wort this way to get your runoff as clear as possible.

Keep sparging until you have collected about 6.5 gallons of sweet wort. You may swap the sparge pot for the mash pot to collect the last portion of the wort, if the mash pot size is too small to hold all the wort. The sparge pot is available for this purpose as soon as you have ladled all its water onto the surface of the grain. You can then, either boil the volumes in two seperate pots, or combine the volume into one kettle that is suitably large.

That's about it. When you've collected the full amount of sweet wort, proceed with your boil. From this point on, the process is nearly the same as for extract brewing. What you've been doing, in fact, is creating your own dilute form of malt extract. The only real difference is that, once you come up to a boil, there is still a protein reaction you want to encourage, so the wort is boiled for a half hour before you start adding hops. Hops are boiled for the same lengths of time as with extract brews.

2. Upward Infusion Mashing. Upward Infusion or temperature programmed mashing is similar to standard infusion, except that the mash water is heated to only 130° F. (54 C.) prior to mashing in. Thus, the initial mash temperature is approximately 120° F. (49 C.). It is held there for around 30 minutes in what has traditionally been called a "protein rest." The temperature is then raised to the "sugar rest" level. From that point forward, procede as with infusion.

Note that sugar producing enzymes are active enough to do a complete starch conversion in the range between 130 and 135° F. (54-57 C.), and that their range of maximum activity is 140-149° F. (60-65 C). You could, therefore, accomplish quite a bit of starch to sugar conversion as you raise the temperature to the level of your sugar rest. This will have an effect on the finished beer and will possibly shorten the length of time that you hold the mash at the sugar rest.

3. Decoction Mashing. Decoction is the third mashing method. It comes to us from the continental European tradition, and is widely used in making lager beers. In this system, temperatures are raised by removing a portion of the mash, heating it to boiling, and then returning it to the rest of the mash, mixing thoroughly. You will need one more kettle than the other mashing methods require (for the second mash tun). Observe also that this type of mash uses a higher water to grain ratio than do the other two.

This can become rather involved, as there are single, double, and triple decoctions, but just for starters, try a single decoction. Mash in 60% of your grain at 120° F. (49 C.) as for an infusion mash, but *using two quarts of water per pound of grain.* Preheat the water to about 125° F. (52 C.) before the grain is added.

The other 40% of the grain should be mashed in at about 158° F. (70° C.), by preheating the water to about 165° F. (74° C.). After steeping for 10 minutes, the smaller batch should be gradually raised to a full boil, stirring constantly, and taking approximately 15 minutes to get there. Maintain a rolling boil for 15 minutes, and then combine this with the rest of the mash, mixing well. Then check the temperature, and adjust if necessary to 154-158 F. (68-70 C.) for your sugar rest. Mash off and sparge in the usual way. Because you are using more water in the mash than other systems require, you should find it necessary to *heat no more than four gallons of sparge water for a five gallon batch.*

Additional Points
Three further things should be noted. First, if you intend to serve your beer cold, you may run into chill haze problems with grain beers unless preventative steps have been taken. The best thing you can do, is store your beer at 30-32° F. (0 C.) for two or three weeks after the end of fermentation. That will solidify (and drop out) the protein which causes the haze, so it can be left behind by siphoning away from the sediment. Also, Dave Miller's *The Complete Handbook of Home Brewing*, (pp. 192-193) reports success using Polyclar AT®. Ale brewers, who serve their brews at cellar temperatures of 55° F. (16 C.) will avoid chill haze.

Also, extract brewers who've moved on to grain sometimes report extracting much more bitterness from their hops than they expected. With all grain beers, the entire wort is boiled, but with their extract beers, they were cutting back, boiling an extra thick mixture, and adding water later. That practice is not only risky in terms of contamination (when unboiled water is used), but boiling a concentrated mixture very significantly reduces hop efficiency.

In fact, the reduction is proportional to the amount not being boiled. If you've been boiling only half your wort volume, for example, you may want to reduce your hops by 50% the first time you try boiling the full amount.

Finally, advanced brewers find that adding lactic acid to the sparge water to lower the pH, has a benificial effect on the yield You might want to experiment with adding a couple of teaspoons of 85% Lactic Acid to your sparge water and compare the results to an untreated version.

All-Grain Recipes

AMERICAN STYLE WHEAT BEER 5 U.S. GAL. (19 LITERS)

5 lbs. (2.3 kilos) Wheat Malt
5 lbs. (2.3 kilos) Lager Malt
2 oz. (57 grams) Munich Malt (Munich 10 *or* 20)
Gypsum to 95 ppm.
Chalk to 150 ppm.
Salt to 15 ppm.
10 IBU Saaz Hops (60 min. boil)
3 IBU Tettnang Hops (30 min. boil)
2 IBU Mt. Hood Hops (2 min. boil)
3/4 cup Corn Sugar
1 pint Lager Yeast Starter

> Mash: 90 minute infusion -150° F., 2.8 gallons water.
> Sparge with 5 gallons 170 ° F. water.
> Starting S.G. 49 - IBU 15

PALE ALE 5 U.S. GAL. (19 LITERS)

9 lbs. (4.1 kilos) Pale *or* Lager Malt
1 lb. (454 grams) Crystal Malt (Caramel 40)
8 oz. (227 grams) Crystal Malt (Caramel 20)
Gypsum to 400 ppm.
Chalk to 120 ppm.
Salt 50 ppm.
21 IBU Northern Brewer Hop (60 min. boil)
4 IBU Perle Hop (30 min. boil)
3 IBU Willamette *or* Golding (dryhopped)
3/4 cup Corn Sugar for priming
1 pint Ale Yeast Starter

> Mash: 90 minute infusion 150 ° F., 2.9 gallons water.
> Sparge with 5 gallons 170 ° F. water.
> Starting S.G. 53 - IBU 28

PORTER 5 U.S. GAL. (19 LITERS)

9 lbs. (4.1 kilos) Pale *or* Lager Malt
2 lbs. (907 grams) Crystal Malt (Caramel 20)
12 oz. (340 grams) Chocolate Malt
Gypsum to 75 ppm.
Chalk to 150 ppm.
Salt to 30 ppm.
30 IBU Nugget *or* Chinook Hops (60 min. boil)
4 IBU Cascade Hops (30 min. boil)
4 IBU Willamette *or* Cascade Hops (dryhopped)
3/4 cup Corn Sugar for priming
1 pint Ale or Stout Yeast Starter

> Mash: 90 minute infusion -155° F., 2.4 gallons water.
> Sparge with 5 gallons 170 °F. water.
> Starting S.G. 50 - IBU 38

NUT BROWN ALE 5 U.S. GAL. (19 LITERS)

8 lbs. (3.6 kilos) Pale *or* Lager Malt
8 oz. (227 grams) Home Toasted Malt (20 min. at 300° F.)
12 oz. (340 grams) Crystal Malt (Caramel 20)
8 oz. (227 grams) Crystal Malt (Caramel 40)
4 oz. (113 grams) Chocolate Malt
Gypsum to 50 ppm.
Chalk to 150-200 ppm.
Salt to 30-50 ppm.
19 IBU Nugget Hop (60 min. boil)
6 IBU Northern Brewer Hop (30 min. boil)
2 IBU Northern Brewer Hop (dryhopped)
3/4 cup Corn Sugar for priming
1 pint Ale Yeast Starter

> Mash: 90 minute infusion -150° F., 2.4 gallons water.
> Sparge with 5 gallons 170 ° F. water.
> Starting S.G. 45 - IBU 27

Dry Stout 5 u.s. gal. (19 liters)

8 lbs. (3.6 Kilos) Pale Malt
1 lb. (454 grams) Roasted Barley
1 lb. (454 grams) Crystal Malt (Caramel 20)
4 oz. (113 grams) Crystal Malt (Caramel 40)
4 oz. (113 grams) Flaked Barley
Gypsum to 75 ppm.
Chalk to 150-200 ppm.
Salt to 30-50 ppm.
42 IBU Nugget Hop (60 min. boil)
4 IBU Willamette Hop (30 min. boil)
4 IBU Golding Hop (dryhopped)
3/4 cup Corn Sugar for priming
1 pint Ale *or* Stout Yeast Starter

> Mash: 90 minute infusion -150° F., 2.4 gallons water.
> Sparge with 5 gallons 170 ° F. water.
> Starting S.G. 53 - IBU 50

German Pils Style Light Lager 5 u.s. gal.

10 lbs. (4.5 kilos) Lager Malt
8 oz. (227 grams) Munich Malt (Munich 10 to 15)
4 oz. (113 grams) Crystal Malt (Caramel 20)
Gypsum to 40 ppm.
Salt to 20 ppm.
24 IBU Mt. Hood *or* Hallertau Hops (60 min. boil)
2 IBU Tettnang Hops (2 min. boil)
1 cup Corn Sugar for priming
1 pint Lager Yeast Starter

> Mash: 90 minute infusion - 150° F., 3 gallons water.
> Sparge with 5 gallons 170° F. water.
> Starting S.G. 52 - IBU 26

Munich Helles Lager 5 u.s. gal. (19 liters)

9 lbs. (4.1 kilos) Two-Row Lager Malt
8 oz. (227 grams) Home Toasted Malt (20 min. @ 300 F.)
4 oz. (113 grams) Munich Malt (Munich 10)
Gypsum to 95 ppm.
Chalk to 130-150 ppm.
Salt to 15 ppm.
10 IBU Spalt *or* Tettnang Hops (60 min. boil)
7 IBU Mt. Hood *or* Hallertau Hops (60 min. boil)
4 IBU Tettnang Hops (5 min. boil)
1 IBU Mt. Hood *or* Hallertau Hops (5 min. boil)
1 cup Corn Sugar for priming
1 pint Lager Yeast Starter

> Mash: 90 minute infusion - 153 ° F., 3 gallons water.
> Sparge with 5 gallons 170 °F. water.
> Starting S.G. 50 - IBU 22

Dortmund Export Lager 5 u.s. gal. (19 liters)

11 lbs. (5 kilos) Lager Malt
8 oz. (227 grams) Munich Malt (Munich 5 to 15)
4 oz. (113 grams) Crystal (Caramel 20)
Gypsum to 225 ppm.
Chalk to 175 ppm.
Salt to 50 ppm.
17 IBU Mt. Hood *or* Hallertau Hops (60 min. boil)
3 IBU Tettnang Hops (5 min. boil)
1 cup Corn Sugar for priming
1 pint Lager Yeast Starter

> Mash: 90 minute infusion -152° F., 3.2 gallons water.
> Sparge with 5 gallons 170 °F. water.
> Starting S.G. 55 - IBU 20

"Octoberfest" Amber Lager 5 u.s.gal.

8 lbs. (3.6 kilos) Lager Malt
2 lbs. (907 grams) Munich Malt (Munich 10 to 15)
1 1/2 lbs. (680 grams) Cara-Pils Malt
1 lb. (454 grams) Munich Malt (Munich 20)
8 oz. (227 grams) Crystal Malt (Caramel 60)
Gypsum to 100 ppm.
Chalk to 100 ppm.
Salt to 75 ppm.
11 IBU Perle Hops (60 min. boil)
6 IBU Mt. Hood Hops
and 1 IBU Tettnang Hops (30 min. boil)
2 IBU Mt. Hood Hops (5 min. boil)
3/4 cup Corn Sugar for priming
1 pint Lager Yeast Starter

> Mash: 90 minute infusion -154° F., 3.6 gallons water.
> Sparge with 5 gallons 170 °F. water.
> Starting S.G. 55 - IBU 20

Munich Dunkel 5 u.s. gal. (19 liters)

9 lbs. (4.1 kilos) Lager Malt
2 lbs. (907 grams) Munich Malt (Munich 10 to 20)
1 lb. (454 grams) Crystal Malt (Caramel 40)
8 oz. (227 grams) Crystal (Caramel 90)
Gypsum to 95 ppm.
Chalk to 150 ppm.
Salt to 15 ppm.
8 IBU Northern Brewer *or* Perle Hops (60 min. boil)
6 IBU Northern Brewer *or* Perle Hops (30 min. boil)
6 IBU Mt. Hood or Hallertau Hops (5 min. boil)
3/4 cup Corn Sugar for priming
1 pint Lager Yeast Starter

> Mash: 90 minute infusion - 154° F.,3.5 gallons water.
> Sparge with 5 gallons 170 °F. water.
> Starting S.G. 50 - IBU 20

OTHER ADVANCED TECHNIQUES

There are a few more areas of home brewing that are worth investigating after you are familiar with the basic procedures. You may have noticed a change in format in the all grain recipe section that preceeds this. The water treatments were given in parts per million (ppm) instead of teaspoons and tablespoons. An explanation for how to fine tune your water follows.

An introduction to grain malts and their contributions to brewing was discussed in the ingredients section of the book, pp. 14-20. In addition to their fementability, grain color is an important component of brewing to style. The section on Standard Research Measure (SRM) will help you adjust your recipe to take color into account. Guidelines for toasting your own malt are also given here.

The last section focuses on the time savings and other benefits of kegging your beer instead of bottling. If you like the fresh taste of draft beer, you'll appreciate the instructions that follow.

USE OF WATER SALTS IN BREWING

Most brewers don't worry about the fine points of water treatment until they become quite advanced. However, those who do venture into this area often find the rewards significant. For several years, I've been working on a chart to help introduce brewers to the topic. Starting with a few published sources, the chart has been refined, over the years, on the basis of experience. This will probably continue, but here's the current version.

Assuming that your water tastes reasonably pleasant, you can normally use it in making beer. Obviously, such problems as a high iron or salt content might require getting water from an alternate source, but in most situations, good tasting water is probably okay. Different types of water supplies, however, will affect your results, either positively or negatively, depending on the type of beer you're trying to make. Historically, the reason a particular city became renowned for a certain type of beer was often because the water supply was especially suitable.

If you're starting with de-ionized or distilled water in your brewing, this table gives you some guidelines for treating the water to make ten gallons of several types of beers. If using tap water, as most of us do, you should test your water, or have it tested, and adjust these amounts accordingly. Note that if you're working with harder water than is appropriate for the style you've selected to brew, you may need to adjust with a percentage of de-ionized, or distilled water.

If you're on a municipal water system, getting the statistics on your water can be relatively easy. You may be able to call your water company and get figures on both the permanent (sulfate) and temporary (carbonate) hardness, as well as the salinity (salt content) of your water.

If working with well water, you can get approximate hardness figures with a water hardness test kit. *Figures in the following tables are given in parts per million (ppm.) for* **10 gallon volumes.**

If adding water salts, use the following tables:
>One gram Gypsum (calcium sulfate) = 21 ppm.
>One gram Salt (sodium chloride) = 27 ppm.
>One gram Chalk (calcium carbonate) = 27 ppm.
>One gram Epsom Salts (magnesium sulfate) = 36 ppm.

If you don't have a gram scale, use the following estimates:
>One tsp. Gypsum = approx. 75-85 ppm.
>One tsp. Salt = approx.130-135 ppm.
>One tsp. Chalk = approx. 85-90 ppm.
>One tsp. Epsom Salts = approx.75-85 ppm.

WATER SALTS FOR COMMON BEER STYLES

Beer Type	Salt	Gypsum	Chalk	Epsom Salts
Classic Pale Ale	50-75	100-450	0-130	0-30*
Bitter	40-70	200-350	0-130	0-30*
India Pale Ale	30-60	75-125	0-130	0-30*
Altbier	70-80	100-150	0-100	
Light Ale	20-40	250-400	0-50	
Cream Ale	20-40	50-100	0-50	
Mild Ale	70-100	80-150	50-100	
Brown Ale	100-150	50-100	50-100	
Scottish Brown	60-80	75-125	80-125	
Sweet Stout	30-50	50-80	150-200	
Porter	30-50	50-80	150-200	
Dry Stout	30-50	70-100	150-200	
Classic Pilsner	5-20	5-20	10-20**	
German Pils	20-30	40-80	**	
American Lager	20-40	60-100	**	
Dortmunder Export	50-70	200-300	175-180	
Munich Helles	60-90	120-180	**	
Vienna/Okt.	75-100	100-200	90-110	
Munich Dunkel	10-30	75-125	130-150	
Bock	100-150	50-80	150-200	
Hellesbock	30-60	60-90	50-100	
Doppelbock	100-180	50-80	150-200	
Rauchbier	50-75	100-150	100-150	
Weizen (light)	20-30	50-100	125-150	
Weizenbock	70-80	50-100	125-150	
American Wheat	20-40	60-100	0-130	

* Optional.
**** If water is high in temporary hardness, boil for 5-10 minutes, and
remove from the settlings before use.**

Standard Research Measure (SRM)

When you, as an advanced brewer, begin imitating the classic beer styles of the world, brewing will remain a creative activity, but in a somewhat more disciplined way than when you started out. Most aspects of this disciplined approach have already been presented during the course of this book.

You will, for example, attempt to match the hop bitterness level of your beer to the style you're attempting to match (See pp. 28-33.) You will also make an attempt to adjust water salts to appropriate levels. The time and temperature sequence of your mash can be shifted around to fine tune your efforts. It remains to briefly discuss malt grains, and how to select them in conformity with stylistic parameters.

If you have analyzed the recipes on pp. 92-96, you will already have noticed that there are a lot more pounds of pale grains than darker ones, even in the darker beers.

One reason is that these pale grains yield the most sugar per pound. The other is that they also contain the enzymes which convert grain starches to fermentable sugar in your mash.

Grain malts with ratings higher than about 20 SRM will generally not contain any active enzymes, and must depend on pale grains in the mash for conversion. The darker "specialty" grains are primarily used for color and flavor, though all but the really black grains will contribute some sugars as well.

As you develop your own recipes, you will, therefore, use primarily pale malts, with just enough specialty malts to get the color you want. The biggest hurdle in learning to match beer styles is to get both the specific gravity and SRM (color) ratings of your batch in line with the guidelines for a particular style.

It may take a few batches to evaluate the efficiency of your mashing and sparging setup, so that the gravity can be properly adjusted. If you take the time to calculate your recipe's SRM rating, however, you ought to have the color pretty close to where you want it in the very first attempt, especially with the lighter beers, where, incidentally, it matters the most.

Here are some suggested Specific Gravity and SRM ranges for some of the world's common beer styles:

Beer	SG	SRM
Classic Pale Ale	44-56	5-10
Bitter	35-55	8-14
India Pale Ale	50-65	4-7
Altbier	44-48	11-19
Light Ale	40-50	3-5
Cream Ale	44-55	3-4
Mild Ale	32-35	17-34
Brown Ale	40-55	17-25
Scottish Brown	40-50	20-30
Sweet Stout	45-55	over 40
Porter	45-60	over 30
Dry Stout	40-50	over 40
Czech Pilsner	48-50	4-4.5
German Pils	45-50	3-4
American Lager	40-50	2-4
Dortmund Export	50-56	4-6
Munich Helles	45-50	3-5
Vienna/Okt.	50-60	8-14
Munich Dunkel	52-56	17-25
Bock	65-75	20-30
Hellesbock	65-70	4.5-7
Doppelbock	75-85	12-30
Rauchbier	48-55	10-20
Weizen	48-55	3-9
Weizenbock	65-80	10-30
American Wheat	35-50	2-8

Calculating the SRM for a Recipe.

For each grain called for in the recipe, you simply multiply the number of pounds of grain by that grain's SRM rating (Your malt supplier should provide ratings for the grain). When you've done that, add the totals together, and divide by the number of gallons. The number you are left with is the SRM rating for that beer. Look at the style guidelines to make sure you fall within the parameters for the style.

For example, let's take the Dortmund Export recipe on page XX. My lager malt is rated at 1.8 SRM, so we multiply 11 (lbs.) x 1.8 = **19.8**.

A half pound (8 oz.) of Munich Malt with an SRM rating of 10 would be .5 x 10 = **5**, and a quarter pound (4 oz.) of Caramel Malt rated at 20 is .25 x 20 = **5** also.

Add the bold numbers together **(19.8 + 5 + 5 = 29.8)**, and divide the answer (29.8) by the number of gallons, five in this case, **(29.8 / 5 = 5.96.)** *That leaves you with a final SRM rating of 5.96 for this recipe, within the accepted color range for Dortmund Export style beers.*

Note that, when calculating these SRM ratings, you should presume a full sugar rest of approximately 90 minutes. Sometimes, you can "finesse" a recipe by cutting back slightly on the time of the mash.

For an easy example, let's say that you wanted to make the Dortmund Export recipe, but the only Munich Malt your supplier has in stock rates at 15 SRM. Factoring that into the equation, instead of the Munich 10, would leave your beer with a final SRM rating of 6.46, a bit high for an Export.

One option, of course, might be to use only four ounces of Munich instead of eight. Let's say, however, that you really like Munich Malt, and don't want to cut back because of the flavor profile it provides. Your second option is to shorten the sugar rest portion of the mash by 15 or 20 minutes. That would give you a lighter "tea" without changing the recipe or interfering with the enzyme reactions of the mash.

Whatever your choice may be in any given situation, being aware of (and working with) the SRM ratings of your grain malts will help you gain additional control over your brewing process.

HOME TOASTING MALT

The idea of taking uncrushed lager malt and toasting it in the oven to extract unique, fresh-roasted aromatics, was mentioned earlier in this book. It's time now to elaborate further on the theme. If adjusting the color of recipes by SRM reflects the disciplined side of home brewing, malt toasting can help you unleash your creative side once again.

The basic process is simple. Spread out some grain malt on a clean cookie sheet or roasting pan (lined, if necessary, with aluminum foil) no more than one inch deep, and toast it in a preheated oven. At the appropriate time, take it out and let it cool. That's all there is to it.

Three variables concern you: time, temperature, and the kind of malt you wish to toast. Changing any of these variables will affect the results.

For example, toasting Lager Malt at 300° F. (149 C.) for only 10 minutes, should give you a malt similar to a light Munich Malt (around 5-6 SRM). Increasing the time to 20 minutes will give you a somewhat darker malt (about 15 SRM). A 20-25 minute toast with the temperature around 350° F. (177 C.) should yield a malt with roughly the same coloring potential as Medium Caramel Malt (SRM 40), but with a very different flavor profile.

You may toast any reasonably light colored malt, and in each case, the effect will vary, so I recommend lots of experimentation.

In most cases, you will want to employ toasting times between 10 and 45 minutes, at temperatures ranging from 300-400 degrees° F. (149-204 C.). The longer the time or higher the temperature, the more color and toasted flavors you will get. *After toasting grain, it is best to wait at least a week for the flavors to mellow prior to use.*

Toasting malt is fun. I've been experimenting with this ever since Charlie Papazian suggested the idea years ago. For further information, I recommend Appendix 1 of *Old British Beers and How to Make Them.* (See Bibliography.)

DRAFT BREWING

Sooner or later, most home brewers consider the question of whether to stop bottling all their brews and invest in a draft beer system. The question arises from a combination of two reasons. They may simply get tired of cleaning bottles. They may also come to the realization that, everything else being equal, draft beer is better than the bottled equivilent.

In my opinion, the best draft containers for home brewers are the stainless steel, five gallon, "soda" or "syrup" kegs used by convenience stores, and other places that dispense soft drinks. The first reason is the size. Five gallons tends to be the normal batch size for most of us, and that makes it almost too easy to resist, especially for those who really want no more bottle washing whatsoever. Three gallon kegs are commonly available as well, for those who want to fit a tight refrigerator space, or who wish to bottle part of a batch (for sending to judgings, etc.)

Commercial half or quarter barrel kegs are harder to carry around than soda kegs. Soda kegs need only a few standard tools, instead of special wrenches, and their "quick disconnect" fittings allow you to make an emergency change when you run out of beer.

Most important of all, though, is the fact that this is an excellent system for draft beer, however you work with it.

One way to carbonate these kegs is to just to treat the keg like a big bottle. In this case, you simply move your beer to the keg after fermentation is finished, and prime it with sugar syrup (using half a cup of corn sugar). Replace the lid and add some CO_2 to the head space to seal the lid. Set it aside for a week or two until your beer has had a chance to fully carbonate. The disadvantage of doing it this way is that you need active yeast in the keg to carbonate the beer, so you're going to be left with a fair amount of sediment, and you'll probably have to cut off the bottom half inch or so of your downtube to avoid having really cloudy beer.

Personally, I prefer to force carbonate my kegs by adding CO_2 instead of priming for three reasons.

First, this practice leaves my keg virtually sediment-free, which means I can leave my downtube uncut, and still draw beautifully clear beer right to the bottom.

Second, if the beer is cold enough at the time of carbonation, the kegs can be fully carbonated in just three days time, instead of several weeks, which comes in handy in emergencies.

Third, the cold box I use for beer storage will hold several soda kegs stacked on their sides like cordwood, but the compartments aren't quite high enough to store the kegs standing up. If they were primed, all the sediment would collect on the side of the keg (rather than the bottom) and drift down, clouding the beer as soon as the keg upright for dispensing. This way, there's only a tiny bit of sediment, even in my unfiltered beer, and the minute amount that does drift down isn't enough to notice.

My Procedure For Force Carbonating Draft Beer.

Prior to this procedure, of course, the beers should have finished fermenting, and been stored in topped-up settling containers, preferably for at least three weeks.

First, sanitize your siphon assembly, thermometer, and keg with an iodophor sanitizer. Replace the keg lid, and jostle the keg around to expose all interior surfaces for several minutes of contact time. Then assemble the carbon dioxide and beverage hoses, with their inlet and outlet disconnect fittings, clamping them into place. Push the sanitizer out through the down tube with CO_2.

Now the keg is clean, sanitized and empty. Remove the lid and shake out any residual sanitizer in the keg. Siphon in the beer, being careful not to pick up sediment from the bottom of the carboy.

When the keg has been filled, use your thermometer to check the exact temperature of the beer. Secure the lid and attach the gas line to the gas ("in") fitting of the keg. Turn on the gas at low pressure (5 psi). Turn off the gas and pull the release vent on the keg. Repeat this sequence four or five times. Each time the keg is vented like this, you are cutting the oxygen content of the airspace by half, and by half again, until, after you've done it several times, you have a relatively pure CO_2 atmosphere.

Rearrange The Disconnect Fittings For Carbonating.

After reducing the oxygen in the keg, remove the gas fitting from the keg, and turn off the gas flow. Replace the normal "in" fitting on the gas line with a beverage ("out") fitting. From the *Carbonation Chart* supplied on page 109, find the temperature of the beer that corresponds to your reading and read across to the CO_2 volume that is appropriate for this beer style. You'll find an additional chart referencing styles on the next page. Now read the pounds per square inch (PSI) that runs across the top of the page and set the screw on your gas regulator clockwise until you reach that level.

As you can see, the chart is a spreadsheet with temperature going down the left side, and PSI going across the top. The volumes of CO_2 go off at an angle between them toward the lower right. The temperature of the beer is what determines how much pressure has to be applied. The chart shows that the warmer the beer is, the more PSI you have to apply to do the job.

Volumes of CO₂ By Beer Style.

Carbonation, is a matter of your own personal taste, and the the style of beer you are making, but here are some general guidelines:

British Style Beers - 2.0 to 2.4
Most Other Beers - 2.4 to 2.85
Highly Carbonated Beers - 2.85 to 2.95

Keep the gas on and rock the keg back and forth. Doing this when the temperature of the beer is about 34 ° F. (1 C.), only takes three minutes of rocking. For those working with beer at 45° F. (7 C.) or so, it can take up to 10 minutes of rocking in order to force in the full amount of gas. You will hear the gas passing through the regulator, just keep rocking until additional rocking does not activate that hissing sound.

Disconnect the keg and put it back in cold storage. I find my beer is generally ready in about three days. Attempting to carbonate warmer beer can take up to 10 days or so. Once the beer is carbonated, it can then be hooked up to the CO_2 dispensing system, and as soon as it reaches a reasonable serving temperature, its ready to tap.

Set Up For Serving Beer.

When your beer is carbonated, and you're ready to begin dispensing it, you must first vent the keg to relieve the head space pressure. Assemble and attach your serving line and spigot, with the liquid disconnect clamped in place. Attach your gas line to the gas disconnect. You may begin pushing the beer out with about

14 PSI. That's a standard commercial practice, and will help you dispense your beer with proper carbonation.

If dispensing with 14 PSI, you should use about four feet of 3/16" I.D. tubing on the beverage line, instead of the more common, and larger diameter 1/4" tubing. If you do have the 1/4" tubing, cut back the dispensing pressure to compensate for the lack of resistance of the larger tubing.

We're dealing with a tricky concept here. The way a brewmaster explained it to me, a few years ago, seemed to make the most sense. "There is a point at which a beer has a sufficient CO_2 content that the carbon dioxide will have a tendency to remain in the beer rather than rush to escape." In other words, if you're drawing a glass of draft beer, and whenever you do, you get mostly foam, the paradoxical cause may well be that you have too little carbon dioxide in the beer (so that it wants to escape all at once), rather than too much, or that you're trying to push the beer out with less PSI than you should be using. Try switching to the smaller diameter, 3/16" tubing to solve any foaming problems.

Moving into draft beer brings you one step closer to the freshest beer possible, and makes your job that much easier. There really is something about the character of real draft beer (not just the way you are freed from washing bottles) that makes a draft system one of the most rewarding ways to enhance your pursuit of the home brewing hobby.

Pounds per Square Inch

Temp (°F)	1	2	3	4	5	6	7	8	9	10	11	12	13	14	15	16	17	18	19	20	21	22	23	24	25	26	27	28	29	30
30	1.82	1.92	2.03	2.14	2.23	2.36	2.48	2.60	2.70	2.82	2.93	3.02																		
31	1.78	1.88	2.00	2.10	2.20	2.31	2.42	2.54	2.65	2.76	2.86	2.96																		
32	1.75	1.85	1.95	2.05	2.16	2.27	2.38	2.48	2.59	2.70	2.80	2.90	3.01																	
33		1.81	1.91	2.01	2.12	2.23	2.33	2.43	2.53	2.63	2.74	2.84	2.96																	
34		1.78	1.86	1.97	2.07	2.18	2.28	2.38	2.48	2.58	2.68	2.79	2.89	3.00																
35			1.83	1.93	2.03	2.14	2.24	2.34	2.43	2.52	2.62	2.73	2.83	2.93	3.02															
36			1.79	1.88	1.99	2.09	2.20	2.29	2.39	2.47	2.57	2.67	2.77	2.86	2.96															
37				1.84	1.94	2.04	2.15	2.24	2.34	2.42	2.52	2.62	2.72	2.80	2.90	3.00														
38				1.80	1.90	1.99	2.09	2.20	2.29	2.38	2.47	2.57	2.67	2.75	2.85	2.94														
39					1.86	1.96	2.05	2.15	2.25	2.34	2.43	2.52	2.61	2.70	2.80	2.89	2.98													
40					1.82	1.92	2.01	2.10	2.20	2.30	2.39	2.47	2.56	2.65	2.75	2.84	2.93	3.01												
41						1.87	1.97	2.06	2.16	2.25	2.35	2.43	2.52	2.60	2.70	2.79	2.87	2.96												
42						1.83	1.93	2.02	2.12	2.21	2.30	2.39	2.47	2.56	2.65	2.74	2.82	2.91	3.00											
43						1.80	1.90	1.99	2.08	2.17	2.25	2.34	2.43	2.52	2.60	2.69	2.78	2.86	2.95											
44							1.86	1.95	2.04	2.13	2.21	2.30	2.39	2.47	2.56	2.64	2.73	2.81	2.90	2.99										
45							1.82	1.91	2.00	2.08	2.17	2.26	2.34	2.42	2.51	2.60	2.68	2.77	2.85	2.94	3.02									
46								1.88	1.96	2.05	2.13	2.22	2.30	2.38	2.46	2.55	2.63	2.72	2.80	2.89	2.98									
47								1.84	1.92	2.00	2.09	2.18	2.25	2.34	2.42	2.50	2.59	2.67	2.75	2.84	2.93	3.02								
48								1.80	1.88	1.96	2.05	2.14	2.21	2.30	2.38	2.46	2.55	2.62	2.70	2.79	2.87	2.96								
49									1.85	1.93	2.01	2.10	2.18	2.25	2.34	2.42	2.50	2.58	2.66	2.75	2.83	2.91	2.99							
50									1.82	1.90	1.98	2.06	2.14	2.21	2.30	2.38	2.45	2.54	2.62	2.70	2.78	2.86	2.94	3.02						
51										1.87	1.95	2.02	2.10	2.18	2.25	2.34	2.41	2.49	2.57	2.65	2.73	2.81	2.89	2.97						
52										1.84	1.91	1.99	2.06	2.14	2.22	2.30	2.37	2.45	2.54	2.61	2.69	2.76	2.84	2.93	3.00					
53										1.80	1.88	1.96	2.03	2.10	2.18	2.26	2.33	2.41	2.48	2.57	2.64	2.72	2.80	2.88	2.95	3.03				
54											1.85	1.93	2.00	2.07	2.15	2.22	2.29	2.37	2.44	2.52	2.60	2.67	2.75	2.83	2.90	2.98				
55											1.82	1.89	1.97	2.04	2.11	2.19	2.25	2.33	2.40	2.47	2.55	2.63	2.70	2.78	2.85	2.93	3.01			
56												1.86	1.93	2.00	2.07	2.15	2.21	2.29	2.36	2.43	2.50	2.58	2.65	2.73	2.80	2.88	2.96			
57												1.83	1.90	1.97	2.04	2.11	2.18	2.25	2.33	2.40	2.47	2.54	2.61	2.69	2.76	2.84	2.91	2.99		
58												1.80	1.86	1.94	2.00	2.07	2.14	2.21	2.29	2.36	2.43	2.50	2.57	2.64	2.72	2.80	2.86	2.94	3.01	
59													1.83	1.90	1.97	2.04	2.11	2.18	2.25	2.32	2.39	2.46	2.53	2.60	2.67	2.75	2.81	2.89	2.96	3.03
60													1.80	1.87	1.94	2.01	2.08	2.14	2.21	2.28	2.35	2.42	2.49	2.56	2.63	2.70	2.77	2.84	2.91	2.98

Temperature of Beer (degrees F.)

Carbonation Chart

Suggested carbonation rates for various beer styles can be found on page 107. To use the chart, look up the temperature of the beer, and read across to the desired level of carbonation. Follow up the line to find what pressure to set your regulator.

Table of Values

Malt and Sugar Values

With one pound of the following ingredients per U.S. gallon of water, you may reasonably expect the following specific gravities. Grain yields, however, will be quite variable, depending on the efficiency of your grinding, mashing, and sparging systems.

Ingredient	Gravity	Ingredient	Gravity
Malt Syrup	1.036	Dry Malt	1.045
Dry Rice Extract	1.045	Corn Sugar	1.036
Cane Sugar	1.045	Brown Sugar	1.045
Rice Syrup	1.036	Dextrin Powder	1.045
Pale Malt	1.030	Lager Malt	1.028
Munich Malt	1.025	Mild Ale Malt	1.028
Caramel Malt	1.020	Wheat Malt	1.028
Dextrine Malt	1.025		

Specific Gravity and Balling Equivalents

Balling	S.G.	Balling	S.G.
0	1.000	13	1.050
1	1.004	14	1.054
2	1.008	15	1.058
3	1.012	16	1.062
4	1.016	17	1.066
5	1.019	18	1.070
6	1.023	19	1.074
7	1.027	20	1.078
8	1.031	21	1.081
9	1.035	22	1.085
10	1.039	23	1.089
11	1.043	24	1.093
12	1.047		

Saccharometer Temperature Correction

Most saccharometers you will encounter are set to read correctly at 60 degrees F. (16 C.). If your sample is not at that temperature, you should correct your observed reading by adding or subtracting gravity points as indicated below.

Degrees C.	Degrees F.	Correction
0	32	Subtract 1.6
5	41	Subtract 1.3
10	50	Subtract .8
16	60	Read as observed
20	68	Add 1.0
25	77	Add 2.2
30	86	Add 3.5
35	95	Add 5.0
40	104	Add 6.8
45	113	Add 8.8
50	122	Add 11.0
55	131	Add 13.3
60	140	Add 15.9

Note that these adjustments are for samples with a specific gravity of 1.040. If your gravity is significantly lower, the corrections needed would be very slightly smaller. If it is significantly higher, the corrections would be slightly larger. It's unlikely, though, that home brewers will ever have to be quite that fine.

Fahrenheit and Celsius

To convert a Fahrenheit reading to Celsius: subtract 32 from the Fahrenheit figure, and divide the result by 1.8.

To convert a Celsius reading to Fahrenheit, multiply the Celsius figure by 1.8, and add 32 to the result.

Weight and Measure Equivalents

Fluid Measure

U.S. System
1 fluid ounce = 2 tablespoons = 29.5729 ml.
1 cup = 8 fluid ounces = 228.6 ml.
1 pint = 16 fluid ounces = 473.166 ml.
1 quart = 32 fluid ounces = 946.332 ml.
1 gallon = 128 fluid ounces = 3.7853 liters
1 liter = 33.8148 fluid ounces = 1000 ml.
Imperial System
1 imperial fluid ounce = .96 U.S. fluid ounce = 28.41 ml.
1 imperial pint = 20 imperial fluid ounces = 568.25 ml.
1 imperial gallon = 160 imperial fluid ounces and
   = 1.2 U.S. gallons = (4.5459 liters)

Weight Measure

1 oz. (avoirdupois) = 28.3495 grams
1 lb. = 16 ounces = .4536 kg. (453.592 grams)
1 kilogram = 2.2046 lbs.= 1000 grams

ANNOTATED BIBLIOGRAPHY

This listing has a twofold purpose. First, it allows me to credit the various writers I've found it helpful to consult when confronted with a technical question on brewing over the years. Many of their insights, both oral and written, have been incorporated into my own brewing, and are, in turn, reflected in this book. Second, it provides a way for me to recommend further study material to my readers for their consideration.

I hope your continued interest in this remarkable hobby will inspire a lifetime of learning and enjoyment. If it does, some of the names listed below will doubtless play a major role in bringing it to pass.

Aidells, Bruce, and Kelly, Denis. *Real Beer and Good Eats*. New York: Alfred A. Knopf, 1992.

Home brewers have led the way in America's rediscovery of the great beer styles of the world, and it didn't take long to generate lots of interest in serving the various styles of beers with the foods that best suited them. This is the best effort I've seen at this special sort of matchmaking, which only became possible in recent years.

Additionally, many dishes discussed are themselves prepared using beers of various types. Other such books will no doubt emerge, but as of now, this is the best.

Anderson, Stanley, with Hull, Raymond. *The Art of Making Beer*. New York: Hawthorne Books, Inc. 1971.

This was one of the first "modern" home brewing books published in North America. Anderson, president of a chain of winemaking and brewing supply shops headquartered in Canada, made a real contribution in the early 1970s. At that time, the book was marred primarily by a tendency to list items by the brand names of his company. The book has some good recipes, nevertheless, but over the years, has become a bit dated.

Berry, C.J.J. *Home Brewed Beers and Stouts*. 5th ed. Ann Arbor: G.W. Kent, 1981.

Home Brewed Beers and Stouts, first published in 1963, is probably the ancestor of us all. It is probably the first modern home brewing text. It helped launch the movement in Britain, which, in turn, launched us. It contains, of course, a number of recipes which home brewers still find of interest.

Broderick, Harold M. (ed.). *The Practical Brewer*. Madison, Wisconsin:The Master Brewers Assoc. of the Americas, 1977.

For the serious brewer moving into commercial literature, here is where you start. This book is a manual for people going to work at commercial breweries, and is a gold mine of information.

Eckhardt, Fred. *The Essentials of Beer Style*. Portland, Oregon: All Brewer Information Service, 1989.

Back in 1970, the first edition of the author's *A Treatise on Lager Beers* (now out of print) was my first brewing text, and later editions were always counted among my source materials. With the appearance of his book on beer styles, Eckhardt makes an important contribution to American home brewing once again. He provides information on gravities, alcohol content, hops and color for many commercial beers, and suggests a useful (and original) classification system.

Fix, George. *Principles of Brewing Science*. Boulder, Colorado: Brewers' Publications, 1989.

Since its appearance, this book has been widely read by both commercial brewers and serious home brewers. Not intended for everyone, it seeks to provide a most informative analysis of the chemistry of brewing. At least one course in high school chemistry would be helpful, but you can still learn a lot of terminology to impress your buddies.

Forget, Carl. *The Association of Brewers' Dictionary of Beer and Brewing*. Boulder, Colorado: Brewers' Publications, 1988.

This book is exactly what it says, a dictionary, but that doesn't tell you how much fun there can be in thumbing through it, reading about all sorts of things having to do with brewing, many of which you've never heard of before. That's another way of saying it's a real educational tool, and enjoyable at the same time.

Harrison, John, *Old British Beers and How to Make Them*. rev. ed. London: The Durden Park Beer Circle, 1991.

This book will charm any brewer with a sense of history. Harrison, along with his fellow clubmembers scoured historical records and brewery archives in an attempt to duplicate old time brews. Besides the invaluable historical information, there are 60 (all grain) recipes for beers dating back as far as 1300

A.D. This delightful book should be owned by all advanced brewers with an interest in British beers.

Hough, J.S., Briggs, D.E., Stevens, R., and Young, T.W. *Malting and Brewing Science*. 2nd ed. London and New York: Chapman and Hall, 1981, 1982.

Without doubt, *Malting and Brewing Science* is the "Bible" of the brewing industry, and has been for years. Only for those who wish to venture deeply into the commercial brewing literature, as it is expensive to purchase and time consuming to read.

Jackson, Michael. *The Great Beers of Belgium*. 2nd ed. Antwerp: M.M.C - CODA, 1992.

Think of this as the Belgian chapter from *The New World Guide to Beer*, held under a powerful magnifying glass to reveal much more detail, causing that one section to grow into an entire book. Don't go to Belgium without reading it.

Jackson, Michael. *The New World Guide to Beer*. Philadelphia: Running Press, 1988.

This is not, of course, a book on brewing, but is instead, an expanded and updated version of Jackson's glorious celebration of beer. It merits inclusion here, not only because it is of major interest to all lovers of beer, but because it will help refine your awareness and understanding of beer styles. That, in turn, will benefit your brewing.

Line, Dave. *Brewing Beers Like Those You Buy*. Ann Arbor: G.W. Kent, 1978.

A renowned British home brewer's attempt to duplicate many of the world's most popular beers.

Line, Dave. *The Big Book of Brewing*. Ann Arbor: G.W. Kent, 1974.

This is the classic work focusing on grain brewing in England. If you are heading toward advanced brewing, you will want to make a lengthy stop here. As you might expect, the emphasis is on ales and stouts.

Loysen, Papazian, and Raizman (eds.). *The Winners Circle*. Boulder, Colorado: Brewers'Publications, 1989.

This useful book provides a selection of prizewinning recipes from the first ten years of the American Homebrewers Association's national competition. The recipes are grouped by style, and accompanied by brief style descriptions. Care has been taken to provide both extract and grain recipes whenever possible.

Mares, William. *Making Beer*. New York: Alfred A Knopf, Inc., 1984.

In brewing, as in life, it's sometimes necessary to stop and do something just for the sheer enjoyment of it. Reading this book (by a Vermont humorist and home brewer) comes under this dictum. It's a homebrewer's odyssey through the hobby, filled with sagacity and good fun. The last part of this book (seriously) is required reading for any home brewer dreaming about starting a commercial brewery. Mares shares the fruits of his research into the question of "going pro," and explains why he decided not to do it. Don't even think about starting a brewery unless you can answer his objections.

Miller, Dave. *Brewing the World's Great Beers*. Pownal, Vermont: Storey Communications, 1992.

This is an accessible introduction to brewing beers specifically to match the world's classic beer styles. This book includes recipes, tips, and a discussion of draft beer, counter-pressure bottling, and filtration. This would be a good third or fourth book to read. The author is brewmaster at the St. Louis Brewing Co.

Miller, Dave. *The Complete Handbook of Home Brewing*. Pownal, Vermont: Storey Communications, 1988.

I have trouble with the suggestion that any book on such an open-ended topic as home brewing should be called complete, and Miller, it must be noted, published a second book four years after this one. However, this book provides a great deal of information useful for both advanced and intermediate brewers. He helps you understand the "whys" of some of the "whats." This would be a good second book to read once you've finished *Brewing Quality Beers*, and have a few brewing sessions under your belt.

Noonan, Gregory J. *Brewing Lager Beer*. Boulder, Colorado: Brewers' Publications, 1986.

This book is the first comprehensive work for advanced home brewers and small commercial brewers with an emphasis on lager beers. The gap between the home brewing and commercial brewing literatures is expertly bridged, providing much needed support for anyone attempting to make the transition.

Impressive as Noonan's technical grasp is, his ability to render difficult topics comprehensible is even more so. Many brewers will find the chapter on water alone to be worth the book's cost, though there is much more here than that. This book is a classic. If you have any aspirations toward advanced brewing, you should own a copy. The author is now owner/brewmaster at The Vermont Brewing Company in Burlington.

Papazian, Charlie. *The New and Complete Joy of Home Brewing.* 2nd Ed. New York: Avon Books, 1991.

Though, once again, I don't really believe a single book will ever be "complete" in the sense of definitive, this book is otherwise aptly named. No one comes to brewing more joyfully, or ambitiously than Papazian, our hobby's foremost ambassador.

This is a large book, packed with information and insight, though it could use a better fermentation method for beginners. Every home brewer should have this one, and should move on to it as soon as the books by Dave Miller have been finished.

The author has done an excellent job of popularizing the use of "specialty" or "novelty" ingredients (fruit, spices, etc.) by American home brewers, a practice that has become widespread in recent years.

Pollock, J.R.A. (ed.). *Brewing Science.* New York: Academic Press, 1979,1981.

This is a weighty, two volome, commercial text for only the most serious. The information, however, is excellent. I believe this may now be out of print, and hard to find.

Vogel, Wolfgang. *Bier aus eigenem Keller.* Stuttgart: Eugen Ulmer, 1984.

Advanced home brewers who read German (or have access to a translator) will enjoy this book, which has lots of ideas on how to adapt traditional German brewing techniques (especially in decoction mashing) for use at home.

In addition to the above works, two series of invaluable books must be mentioned. Both are published in Boulder, Colorado, by the folks at Brewers' Publications.

For some years now, transcripts of the oral presentations at the American Homebrewers' Association's annual conferences have been published under the general title, *Best of Beer and Brewing.* Publication is normally late in the year, and some of the early volumes have now gone out of print.

In 1990, a "Classic Beer Style Series" was initiated, and eight volumes have appeared thus far, each devoted to a different style of beer. These volumes are essential reading material for any brewer wishing to bone up on a particular style. More styles will be explored in future releases.

In addition there are several good magazines that have been a great boon to home brewers.

"Zymurgy." Boulder, CO: The American Homebrewers' Association.

The temptation to call *"Zymurgy"* magazine "the last word in home brewing periodicals" is, unfortunately, irresistible. Nonetheless, the designation is accurate in every sense. The journal of the American Homebrewers Association, it has become a first class magazine, eagerly awaited by home brewers around the world. Published quarterly, with one additional special "theme" issue per year, it speaks to a wide variety of topics interesting to home brewing, with recipes, advice and do it yourself projects.

"Brewing Techniques." Eugene, OR: New Wine Press.

New to the brewing scene in 1993, the first issues of this bi-monthly publication address the more advanced brewer's information needs. Experts from the academic and microbrewing scene, join with notable homebrew authorities on topics of timely importance.

"American Brewer." Hayward, CA: American Brewer Inc.

Editor Bill Owens has been a pioneer in the microbrewing movement with the opening of his Buffalo Bill's Brewpub in 1982. This quarterly publication takes a serious look at the changes taking place to the "Business of Beer", including openings and closings of pubs and microbreweries. Current event articles cover beer styles and organized tastings; and travel pieces cover the American brewing scene.

*"All About Beer."*Durham, NC: Chautauqua, Inc.

Redesigned in 1993, this 14 year-old publication has recently been purchased by Daniel Bradford, a veteran of the home brewing movement. Published semi-monthly, *"All About Beer"* is a magazine for beer lovers of all persausions. It brings an educational slant to beer reviews and a strong commitment to the politics of keeping brewing and beer drinking legal and accessible to all North Americans.

INDEX

BIOGRAPHY

Byron Burch is internationally recognized as a home brewing and winemaking expert, and has taught these arts since 1972.

His first book, *Quality Brewing*, was a major influence in the growth of the American home brew movement during the 1970's and early 1980's. *Brewing Quality Beers* replaced it in 1986.

He has addressed the national conferences of the American Homebrewers' Association and the Home Wine and Beer Trade Association, and had articles published in *"Zymurgy"* magazine, *"Celebrator Beer News," "All About Beer," "The Moderation Reader,"* and *"Practical Winery & Vineyard."*

Winner of numerous awards at the national level, Burch carried off the American Homebrewers' Association's "Homebrewer of the Year" award in 1986, was the national competition high point scorer in both 1986 and 1988, and "Meadmaker of the Year" in 1992.

He owns **The Beverage People**, a brewing and winemaking supply company in Santa Rosa, California and is currently working on a book for home wine and meadmakers.